The House of God

*Places of worship
express the permanence and variety of
religious faith around the world*

The House of God

by *Marion Geisinger*
Introduction by Martin E. Marty

A Ridge Press Book | A&W Publishers, Inc., New York

✳

Editor-in-Chief: Jerry Mason
Editor: Adolph Suehsdorf
Art Director: Harry Brocke
Managing Editor: Marta Hallett
Associate Editor: Ronne Peltzman
Art Associate: Nancy Mack
Art Associate: Liney Li
Art Production: Doris Mullane
Production Consultant: Arthur Gubernick

First published in the United States of America in 1979 by
A & W Publishers, Inc.
95 Madison Avenue
New York, New York 10016
By arrangement with The Ridge Press, Inc.

Library of Congress Catalog Card Number: 79-51842
ISBN: 0-89479-052-8
Printed in The Netherlands

To Robert G.

Contents

Introduction

Surely in temples made with hands,
God the Most High, is not dwelling,
High above earth His temple stands,
All earthly temples excelling . . .

The very idea of houses of God seems to be a contradiction in terms. Whatever else the word "God" points to, it certainly suggests a power or being without limits. Yet a house of any sort does limit; it walls in and rules out, it confines and defines space.

Many religions have hymns comparable to the one above. Yet those who sing such songs still erect excellent temples. They have done so for ages, always aware of limits of their efforts. The Hebrew Scriptures record King Solomon, after he built his temple, pondering: "But will God indeed dwell on earth? Behold, heaven and the highest heaven cannot contain thee; how much less this house which I have built!" (I Kings 8:27). Solomon's temple replaced a bare rock where Jebusites had offered burnt offerings; fissures in the rock caught the blood of sacrifice. When Romans destroyed the second Jewish temple there, they erected a sanctuary to Jupiter Capitolinus. The Moslems, in their turn, replaced this with the Dome of the Rock, believing that its location on Mount Moriah marks the spot whence Muhammad took off for a night journey into heaven.

Jebusites, Jews, Romans, and Moslems all have crowded one rock. Other people of different faiths have built thousands of temples at various times and places. We have to assume that many of them were and are people of intelligence who do wrestle with contradictions. Only a few of them have it easy building a house of God, because they believe their deity is a small homemade object who occupies a bit of space in the shelter they provide. Most other worshipers call such objects idols, and claim that their God is not confinable. What do they think happens when they build a house of God?

In some religions a shrine indicates the presence of the deity, and the building is a symbol of divine reality. In others, people locate their structures where they want to remember a visit to earth of divine beings or some event in the life of

8

their gods and their people. A sacred building may exist to house a relic, some earthly object touched and graced by contact with something or someone sacred. And in certain faiths the builders and users are very explicit: they erect not houses of God at all but merely houses of prayer, where people gather their thoughts without claiming a divine presence.

In every case, something religious goes on in these set-aside spaces. Defining religion is almost as difficult as confining deity, but at the very least something of this sort goes on: the human "feels that some power is bearing down on him" and in turn "he believes he must do something about divine powers who have done something about him" (Professor Julian N. Hartt). Humans seek locales where they can "do something," which usually means some sort of transacting with the divine. In the house of God they pursue what philosopher William James called a "sense of reality, a feeling of objective presence, a perception of what we may call 'something there.'"

Once a temple is somewhere, people may use it to sacrifice to the gods. Others make pilgrimages from ordinary home-bound life to be in contact with extraordinary powers and presences. They may do no more than meditate and they may do much more than dance. The people that moderns call primitive often needed no more than a space under the skies for such activities. Thus some prehistoric Americans formed earthen mounds, giant enclosures, or rude shelters. As much as those who followed them by building cathedrals, they felt a need to rule out the space we call profane, which literally means "before, or beyond, the temple." Worshipers picture leaving such sacred space to return to mundane life renewed by their transactions.

As with sacred space, so with time. Temples beckon people at special hours.

They mark the passages of their own lives in the house of God, seeking divine sanction at the time of their children's births, their own marriages, their burials, to be "hatched, matched, and dispatched," as a less-than-reverent European critic put it. People of prayer like to engage in the same rite in the same season each year, or on the same day of the week at marked hours. Then, having sanctified time, they can again return to ordinary living.

If all people agreed on the uses of the houses of God, this could be a very specialized book, or a very boring one. But even the most casual pager-through should be dazzled at the variety of concepts and accomplishments represented here. Just as some musicians can read a musical score and "hear" it as they go along, so experts in architecture and the study of religion can look at photographs like these or study floor plans of sacred buildings and "see" the beliefs of the people who use them.

Recent Roman Catholicism is one example of change within a tradition, a change reflected in floor plans. Before the Second Vatican Council (1962–65), Catholic churches located the sacred mystery on an altar against a wall distant from the faithful. The new plans place the sacred table toward the midst of the people, to suggest that the mystery is among them. As their Gospel says, "The Word became flesh and tented among us."

For some, the floor plan and building styles suggest the tent, one prototype of sacred architecture for the people of God on the march. The viewer will find here just as many elaborations on another basic model, the cave. There worshipers can withdraw from distraction and find symbolic security with their fellows and their divine protectors.

For centuries critics and prophets have scorned temples or predicted their demise. People of conscience sometimes complain that the cost of buildings diverts funds from bread needed for the poor. Skeptics have foreseen the day when the religious impulse would die, when the last knee would bow in a house of worship, when the last sacred building would become a museum—as some in this book already have.

The prophets, in part, were wrong. Affluent and hedonistic societies may now invest their resources in Superdomes for the new religion of athleticism, or in commercial towers of the sort that dwarf St. Patrick's cathedral in New York. Yet even in modern America more citizens attend church than professional sporting events, and a significant number use houses of God in order to find meaning in their distracted lives. Along with the many ancient temples in this book are numerous evidences of the burst of creativity by our contemporaries, who have not left behind the impulse to react to divine powers.

Since the purposes of these temples not only often coincide but also contradict each other, it is not possible for us to appreciate them all in the same way. We feel mentally at home with the photographs of some and are put off by others. Sometimes we may be like tourists, who gasp our brief appreciations and then move on. Voyeurs, we look over the shoulders of exotic peoples and muse over their esoteric activities. Scholars and critics among us can analyze the transactions. But it is hard to imagine the thoughtful peruser not being moved by the examples before us of humans struggling to ennoble their lives. Whatever else these buildings may be, they are testimonies to the sense of awe that people can feel. They may not tell us all we want to know about the gods, but they reveal something of the scope of art and the depth of the human struggle and achievement.

Martin E. Marty

11

On the summit of a hill overlooking Florence's Piazzale Michelangelo is one of the loveliest of all Italian Romanesque

San Miniato al Monte

churches, San Miniato al Monte. The church is said to stand over the ancient shrine of Miniatus, a Roman soldier who converted to Christianity and was subsequently beheaded by Emperor Decius in 250. In the eleventh-century crypt below the church lie the bones of the saint, Florence's first martyr.

Built in 1013, San Miniato is a simple, beautifully proportioned basilica. Although stone vaults were being developed at the time, Rome's tradition of timber roofing was continued at San Miniato. The green and white marble veneer established the style of alternating colors as a decorative device in Tuscany. The Chapel of the Miraculous Crucifix, a superb Renaissance tabernacle, was built by the noted Florentine architect Bartolomeo Michelozzo in 1448 for Piero de' Medici to house the crucifix of St. Giovanni Gualberto. The saint, an eleventh-century knight, so the story goes, was on his way to San Miniato one Good Friday when he passed the murderer of one of his followers. Instead of taking revenge, Gualberto continued on into the church. As he entered, the figure of Christ on the "Miraculous Crucifix" bowed his head, as if in recognition of Gualberto's merciful act.

In the chapel there are notable glazed terra cotta tiles by Luca Della Robbia. The cloisters contain frescoes by Paolo Uccello, whose fanatical interest in perspective is evident in these works. Giorgio Vasari, in his *Lives of the Great Artists,* remarked that this obsession was so intense that when the artist's wife called him to bed, he simply replied, "Oh, what a sweet thing this perspective is."

13

Bicolored marble façade, first of its kind in Tuscany. Above: Detail of 12th-century ambo.

Left: View of nave shows lavish use of marble in interior.

Michelozzo's Chapel of the Miraculous Crucifix.

Detail of ambo, desk from which Epistles were read.

15

In 1793 a revolutionary mob in Paris celebrated the "Age of Reason" by pulling down all twenty-eight statues on the west *Notre Dame*

front of Notre Dame. Bells and reliquaries went to the smelter. What couldn't be moved was smashed. No one today looking at the graceful flying buttresses or the rose windows can easily imagine the vandalism of the decade called "the Terror."

Twelfth-century Paris, as seat of the monarchy in a kingdom recently unified under the Capet kings, had grown in wealth and power but had only two ancient basilicas. In 1163, Maurice de Sully, bishop of Notre Dame, decided to raise a cathedral worthy of the capital on the Île de la Cité in the Seine.

Notre Dame is the first truly monumental Gothic cathedral in France. It has the first true flying buttress, and the west front is considered one of the world's supreme compositions. Although spires were planned for the twin towers, the harmony of the façade persuaded its unknown master to leave them unfinished. It is still the classic Gothic front with a rose window, the largest of its time, and below it triple sculptured portals. Here tourists and pilgrims still enter as they have for centuries from the medieval forecourt, where a slab marks the spot from which road miles are measured to the ends of France. Built to the glory of the Virgin, most of the rose windows and cathedral portals are decorated in her honor.

That these glories remain is almost miraculous. Over the centuries, horrible destruction was wrought on the "Aged Queen of French cathedrals," as Victor Hugo called her. In the nineteenth century, the old despoiled "Queen" was restored by the architect Viollet-le-Duc.

Flying buttresses (left) and gargoyles (above) are best-known exterior features.

Left: Chandelier is set ablaze by light entering from rose window.

Celebration of mass.

Young worshipers at prayer.

19

Trinity Episcopal Church

Henry H. Richardson's Trinity Church, the most important religious structure in America in the second half of the nineteenth century, not only assured the reputation of its architect, but established a style that revolutionized American architecture.

Characterized by Richardson as a "free rendering of the French Romanesque," Trinity was organized around a great central tower that was, said the architect, "as it were the church itself." To suit the unwieldy, triangular site on the east side of Boston's Copley Square, Richardson adopted a compact cruciform plan, with arms of equal length, the entrance placed broadside across the point of the triangle.

Topped by a pyramidal central tower with an octagonal red-tiled roof, Trinity's chief feature was inspired by a picture postcard sent to Richardson of the tower of Salamanca's cathedral. Contrasting stones—yellow-gray granite with a trim of red sandstone—provide the colorful effect popular in the late Victorian era. The interior, decorated by painter John La Farge, fulfilled Richardson's dream of Trinity as "a colour church." Highlighted by golds and blue-greens against a terra-cotta base and enhanced by La Farge's stained-glass window, the interior glows with a vividness that brings to mind Venice's Saint Mark's.

Richardson's church is a monument to his age and a signal event for the future. In his undisguised use of raw materials and his respect for the unity of form and function, Richardson laid the groundwork for a mode of building that would flower in the works of Louis Sullivan and Frank Lloyd Wright.

21

Freely rendered French Romanesque on a triangular site.

The great church of St. Bavo, towering over the market square in Haarlem, is considered one of the Gothic masterpieces

Great Church of St. Bavo

of the Netherlands. The Gothic style, as exemplified by French Gothic, hardly exists in the Netherlands, and where its influence was felt in the northern provinces, it became less ornate and more severe. The reasons for this may have been purely practical: the reclaimed sea land on which these churches were built could not support the enormous weight of stone vaults, so wooden adaptations were developed. At St. Bavo, which was begun in the fifteenth century, the decorative possibilities of wood were fully exploited. The cedar-ribbed vault at this Haarlem church is one of the finest examples of this evolution.

After the Reformation, major alterations were made as liturgical needs changed. The high altar was destroyed and, in its place, a tablet was affixed to the wall on which was inscribed, in Dutch, the Institution of the Lord's Supper. The choir was rebuilt as a room in which the congregation shared the communal Lord's Supper around long tables. In the nave, the pulpit became the focal point in accordance with Protestant interest in unifying congregation and preacher. The pulpit, built in 1679, is St. Bavo's highlight. A sculptured masterwork, it is surrounded by a copper railing on which are carved fantastic figures.

Dominating the eastern end of the church is St. Bavo's famous organ, built in 1735 by Chrétien Mulder. Here the composer Frederick Handel, performed, as did the young Mozart at the age of ten. Buried at St. Bavo are some of the Netherlands' greatest artists, including Van Osted and Frans Hals.

23

Dutch Gothic is less ornate, more severe. Above: Organ loft.

More than five hundred years after St. Augustine of Canterbury became "bishop of the English," Henry II put Thomas à

Canterbury Cathedral

Becket in the bishop's seat. To Henry, who wanted a pliant tool in the struggle between church and state, it must have seemed unlikely that Becket, a friend of his earlier, wilder days, would become a staunch defender of church rights. One day in 1170, brooding on Becket's resistance, Henry reputedly shouted, "Will no one rid me of this low-born priest?" Four henchmen murdered Becket in the north transept of Canterbury cathedral. That event made Becket a saint. The church had gained a formidable weapon in its fight against secular power. A Becket cult flourished. By the fourteenth century, a pilgrimage to Canterbury was only slightly less important than one to Rome or the Holy Land and was immortalized by Geoffrey Chaucer in his *Canterbury Tales.*

   Little of Becket's church remains. Most of it was destroyed by fire in 1174. To rebuild the gutted choir, Canterbury's chapter hired William of Sens, a French master, who introduced the French Gothic pointed arch. Before it was completed, he fell from a scaffold, suffering an injury that forced his return to France. Work continued under the supervision of William the Englishman, who added the Trinity Chapel, to which Becket's shrine was moved in 1220.

   Nothing remains of the shrine. By 1538 Henry VIII had pronounced Becket a traitor, and the tomb was despoiled. Of the tide of pilgrims coming to Canterbury over 350 years, only worn hollows remain in the famous Pilgrims Steps, and in the vacant rotunda of Trinity Chapel two indentations made by the knees of the faithful.

West front of Becket's church. Above: Heraldic detail.

Perspective view of lovely fan-vaulting.

Thomas à Becket.

Saint's tomb in 13th-century glass.

26

The Dome of the Rock, built in Jerusalem by the caliph Abd-al-Malik in 691, is Islam's most ancient mosque. It dominates the Haram Ash-Sharif, a platform that covers a plot of ground held sacred by the world's three major monotheistic faiths—Judaism, Christianity, and Islam. Here Abraham was ready to offer Isaac in sacrifice, and Solomon's temple stood. From this stone Christ is said to have preached a sermon, and Muhammad flew here from Mecca on his winged horse al-Burak before his ascent to heaven.

Dome of the Rock

The Dome was built after the death of Muhammad, at a time when rival Moslem factions fought for control of the Islamic world. The rule of the Omayyad caliphs, enthroned at Damascus, was threatened by rebellion in the holy cities of Mecca and Medina. In an attempt to lure pilgrims away, the caliph determined to erect a magnificent temple. Aware of the attraction of the great domed Church of the Holy Sepulcher nearby, the caliph ordered his architects to put up a shrine that would rival any temple in Islam and also assert the primacy of Muhammad's beliefs.

The most spectacular decorative element is the Dome's interior, a glittering mosaic of delicate arabesques and calligraphic designs in reds, yellows, and golds. In the sixteenth century, Suleiman the Magnificent replaced the exterior mosaics that had weathered poorly with magnificent Persian tiles in various hues of turquoise, blue, white, and brown, intricately patterned with diamonds, stars, and stylized floral designs. Although the Dome of the Rock is the third holy site of Moslem pilgrimages, after Mecca and Medina, it remains the greatest surviving example of Islamic art.

29

Islam's oldest mosque shelters spot sacred to three major faiths.

Left: Rock of Christ, Abraham, and Muhammad.

Intricate beauty of ceiling.

8th-century Persian tiles.

31

Perched on a hill over-looking the plain of the Saône River in the heart of France, this extraordinary church stands on ground to which pilgrims have made their way for centuries. Designed in 1950 by Le Corbusier to replace a chapel destroyed in World War II, Notre Dame du Haut, the architect wrote, was meant to be "a place of silence, of prayer . . . of spiritual joy," a space reflecting his often-expressed mystical concept of "all-embracing mathematics" as the divine inspiration for its form.

Notre Dame du Haut

Notre Dame, with its silolike tower and enormous, projected roof, at first appears strange and futuristic. The traditional church façade has vanished and the concept of "four walls and roof" has been abandoned for a figure resembling a piece of abstract sculpture. Although the structure is made to appear deceptively simple by a few rustic touches, such as tawny eaves and stuccoed, whitewashed walls, its form is complex, based on modular units by which space is contained and subdivided. The roof, in which some have seen a nun's coif or cresting wave, was in fact, according to Le Corbusier, inspired by a crab shell.

No part of the church's interior, it is said, contains a straight line. Walls curve, the ceiling curves, even the floor inclines, directing the eye toward the great white Burgundian stone altar. Since Notre Dame is a pilgrimage church, twice a year the great enameled steel door swings open to unite the outside sanctuary with the inner sanctum. In his letter to the archbishop on its consecration, Le Corbusier wrote, "I give this chapel of dear faithful concrete in the hope that it will seek out . . . in those who climb the hill, an echo of what we have drawn into it."

33

Wedding party (above) is walking toward end of curved wall (left).

A light in the night at Ronchamp.

Celebration of midnight mass.

34

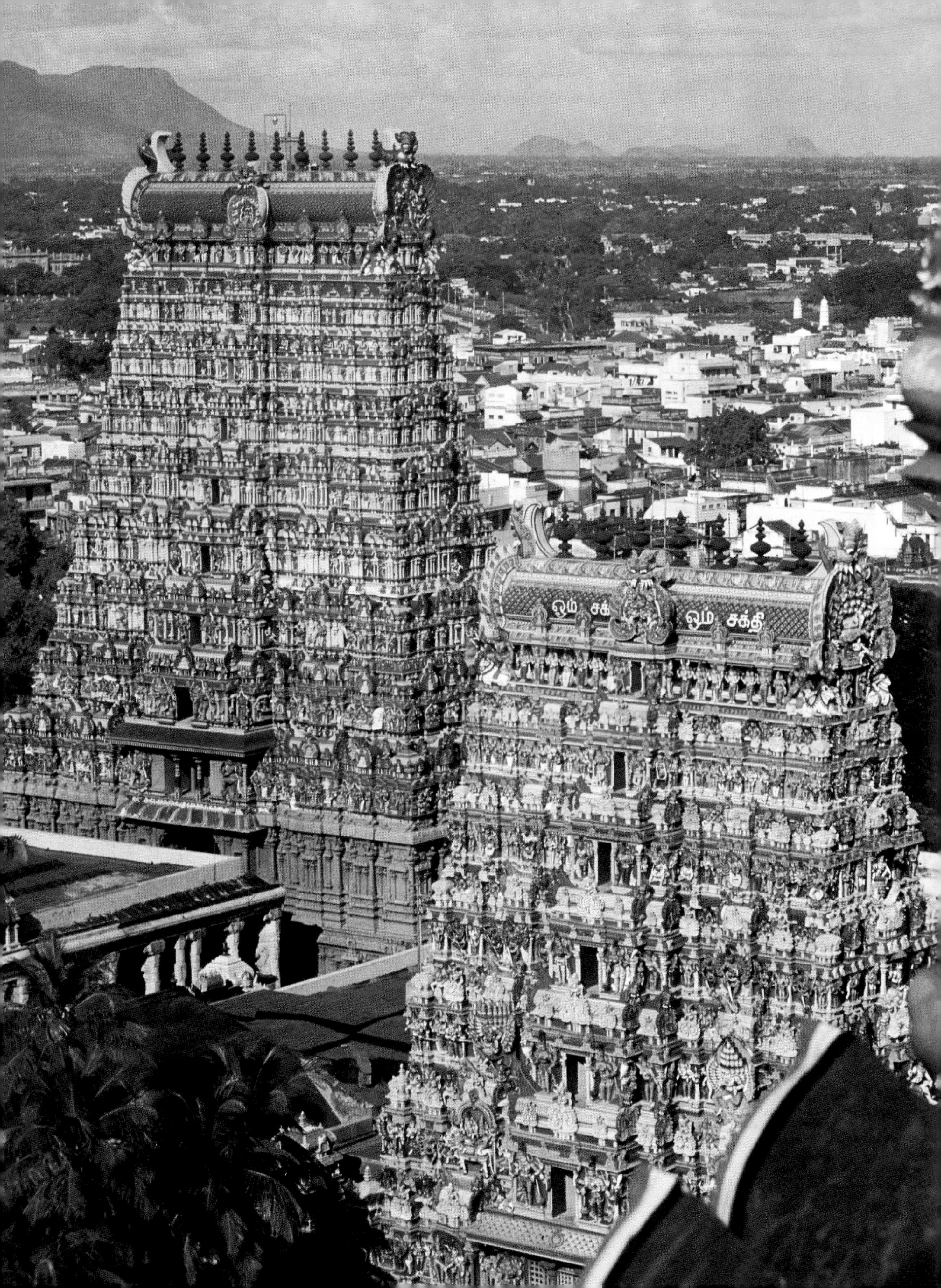
ஓம் சக்
ஓம் சக்தி

One of the finest examples of Dravidian, or south Indian, architecture is found in the Minakshi temple complex in Mad-

Minakshi Temple

urai, Tamil Nadu. It was built by Tirumala Nayaka, the mightiest ruler of the Nayak dynasty, a dominant line of princes reigning in southern India during the sixteenth and seventeenth centuries.

The temple consists of a succession of walled enclosures, the outermost with four gateways at the cardinal compass points over which tower pylons called *gopurams,* and a sequence of pillared halls, or *mandapas,* leading to the inner sanctuaries. The *gopuram* has assumed gigantic proportions at Madurai, the southern tower rising 170 feet. Thousands of sculptured deities of the Hindu pantheon enrich the surface of each of these tapering pyramidal structures. With nine *gopurams* in all, the towers contain 33 million carvings in stone and stucco. Another magnificent feature of the Minakshi temple is its Hall of a Thousand Pillars, noted especially for the carving of Ganesh, the elephant-headed god of good fortune, at the entrance.

At the center of the temple complex is a double sanctuary, one dedicated to Shiva, Lord of the Cosmic Dance of Creation, and the other to one of his favorite consorts, the goddess Minakshi. A major attraction of the Great Temple is the Pool of the Golden Lotus, an artificial lake in which is reflected the towering southern *gopuram.* According to legend, the pool was once used to judge the merit of literary works. Those manuscripts that floated were deemed worthy. Those that sank deserved their fate. For a ten-day period every spring pilgrims crowd into Madurai to celebrate the festival that reenacts the marriage of Lord Shiva to Minakshi.

37

Soaring Dravidian gopurams *reached fullest flowering at Madurai. Above: The goddess Minakshi.*

Left: Detail of gopuram.

Ornately carved figures cover nearly every surface at Madurai, both interior (above) and exterior.

39

In 1385, when Gian Galeazzo Visconti III seized control of Milan and became its first duke, he dreamed also of becoming *Milan Cathedral* the first king of Italy. And as with all men of power, he dreamed of founding a line. To ensure a male heir, Galeazzo decided to build a cathedral as a votive offering, one that would rival the greatest churches of Europe.

Milan's cathedral is Italy's largest Gothic church, and, after Seville, the largest in the world. Unlike its northern Gothic counterparts, which were built solely of stone, Milan's cathedral is unique in its marble casing. The Candoglia marble that clothes it, taken from the duke's quarry, is a creamy-hued stone that, despite centuries of grime, reflects color changes, turning orange, mauve, pink, and violet in turn at sunset. Galeazzo granted the church perpetual rights to the family's quarry, and to this day marble is used to patch the cathedral's fabric.

The eastern end, considered the loveliest part of the church, blends grandeur and beauty in three of the largest windows in the world, the central one bearing the heraldic sign of the Viscontis: a sun with serpentine rays. More than 2,245 statues cover the façade, and on the roof is a forest of 135 pinnacles, a saint's figure standing atop each one. More than fifty architects and sculptors worked on the immense structure between 1386 and 1485, but it took five centuries before it was completed. The bronze doors were finally hung in 1927.

Over the west doors is inscribed a dedication to Mary in these unusual words: *Mariae Nascenti,* "To Mary, the Mother of God who brought the Savior into the world"—Galeazzo's plea for a son.

41

Tracery on vaults is painted, not carved. Above: Delicate swirls of Visconti emblem on window.

Saints perch on 135 pinnacles of world's second largest Gothic church.

This most famous and distinguished synagogue of the seventeenth century became the "mother synagogue" of the western

Portuguese Synagogue

Sephardim, Jews of Portuguese and Spanish ancestry. It is "the glory of Amstel," wrote a Dutch contemporary and a broadside survives showing the fashionable world of Amsterdam attending the grand opening of the new *esnoga,* or synagogue, in 1675.

The Sephardim were mostly Marranos, Iberian Jews who had contrived to cling to the old faith in secret while professing Catholicism openly. Despite their conversion they were hounded by the Inquisition. Many fled to other parts of the Continent, some to the New World, others to North Africa. When Holland threw off the Spanish yoke in 1572 and welcomed the Jewish refugees, Amsterdam became a haven for the Marranos. By 1639, three small Sephardic communities had united. When the *esnoga* became too small for its congregation, 650 members donated the site of the present temple.

The new synagogue, designed by Elias Bouman, an Amsterdam master builder, was modeled after the old one, though on a larger and grander scale. Basically, it is a galleried hall with a large nave supported by twin rows of four large Tuscan columns and twelve slender columns under the galleries. Men sat on benches on the main floor, women in the galleries. The interior has a classical severity, due largely to the prohibition against "graven images." Decoration is lavished instead on the fittings and ceremonial objects and on the woodwork, glass, and metal.

45

Large windows flood synagogue with light. Above: Wedding ceremony.

Men sit below, women in galleries. Tuscan columns are main support of classically severe nave.

46

The gorgeous cathedral of St. Basil the Blessed, on the south end of Moscow's Red Square, is one of the stranger and more eccentric churches ever built. Brilliantly polychromatic and adorned with eight onion-shaped domes clustered around a tentlike spire, its seeming capriciousness is in fact the culmination of a native style of architecture. Originally Byzantine, this style reached its peak in sixteenth-century Russia.

St. Basil's was built by Ivan the Terrible in 1553 to celebrate his military victories over the cities of Kazan and Astrakan, which freed the Grand Duchy of Moscow from centuries of Tartar domination. So brilliant was the execution of this fantasy in stone that Ivan reportedly had his two architects blinded so that they would not repeat their extraordinary achievement.

The cathedral is a complex of nine auxiliary churches joined by a maze of narrow passages surrounding the central church. Eight commemorate the czar's victories. The ninth was added in 1588 to house the remains of St. Basil, Moscow's "holy beggar," who, according to legend, aped idiocy by walking barefoot in the snow to denounce Ivan's monstrous cruelty.

Basically, the ground plan is cruciform; the central church, below which lies the shrine of St. Basil, is surrounded on its four cruciform arms by secondary churches, and by four more at the end of each diagonal line. A unique Russian feature is the "tented roof," pyramidal in form, surmounted by a small, bulbous cupola. The onion-shaped domes developed over the years when the huge Byzantine domes collapsed under the weight of heavy snows.

Cathedral of St. Basil the Blessed

49

Fantastic onion domes give St. Basil's a Byzantine look. Above: Newlyweds in Red Square.

Exterior reflects exuberance of Russian folk art.

51

When Emperor Constantine raised Christianity to equal status with other religions in 313, the era of monumental Christian architecture began. Early Christian churches were of two types. The first, the basilica, was rectangular with long rows of columns separating the nave from the side aisles. The other type, the circular church, consisted of a circular or octagonal area surrounded by an ambulatory. Both types were lit from above.

Santa Costanza

Santa Costanza is the earlier of Rome's two surviving circular churches. Built circa 330 by Constantine as a mausoleum for his daughter, it stands near the basilica of St. Agnes. According to legend, Costanza had fallen gravely ill. Hearing of a miraculous vision at the tomb of the Blessed Agnes, she went there and was cured. The sixth-century *Liber Pontificalis* tells us that "Constantine built the basilica in honor of the holy martyr, to comply with the wish of his own daughter."

Santa Costanza holds within its walkway, or ambulatory, some of the best-preserved fourth-century Christian mosaics in existence. Four holes in the central slab of the rotunda are said to represent insets where the dais stood that held St. Costanza's sarcophagus. By 1256, when the building was formally converted to a church, the casket had begun a strange odyssey. Moved from its venerable center space as the structure became first a baptistery and then a church, it was later expropriated by two popes: Paul II (1464–71) to decorate the front of his Venetian palace, then Paul III (1534–49). So great, however, were the public protests and the complaints of the church canons over the loss of their treasured sarcophagus that in 1788 Pius VI ordered it taken to the Vatican Museum, where it now rests.

Traces of ancient frescoes remain on walls and ceiling. Above: Circular exterior.

One of the triumphs of Persian architecture is the royal mosque of Masjid-i-Shah in Isfahan begun by Abbas the Great in

Masjid-i-Shah

1612. The mosque was skillfully built at an oblique angle to its entrance on the Royal Square of Isfahan, in order to maintain the proper orientation, facing Mecca.

The Shah Abbas was a zealous but impatient builder. Many of the buildings erected during his reign showed early signs of deterioration because of their hasty construction. On one occasion Abbas unreasonably ordered the architect of the Masjid-i-Shah to begin work on the walls before the foundations were laid. Despite incurring the Shah's ire, the architect laid out the foundation and then discreetly went into hiding. When he reappeared, his judgment having been proved sound, a rapprochement was effected with the Shah and building proceeded.

A classic mosque, characterized by four arched *iwans*—vaulted portals—Masjid is built around a square courtyard with a central ablution pool. The hemispherical dome of turquoise faïence tile, the largest and most graceful of its kind, seems to color the entire city. The tiles, patterned with abstract and delicate calligraphic designs, became the predominant external fabric of the mosque. They were created through an elaborate process of preparing plaster and then brilliantly glazing it in one color, usually ultramarine, turquoise, or white. In contrast, the interior was decorated with *hafti rangi,* or seven-colored painted tiles, which lacked the brilliance of the faïence on the outside. Within the main portal the half dome is filled with stalactite decoration, characteristic of Islamic buildings, and a calligraphic frieze praising Allah and Abbas the Great.

55

Graceful dome of faïence. Above: "Stalactite" decoration inside.

Mosque is skillfully built on angle for proper orientation to Mecca.

On a bluff overlooking the River Tarn in southwestern France stands the magnificent red brick cathedral of Albi, rising imperiously over the hillside. In this peaceful setting occurred one of the grimmest episodes in European history, the suppression of the Albigensian heresy.

Albi Cathedral

An ascetic Christian sect calling itself the Cathari, whose members disavowed all Catholic doctrine, had settled in and around Albi in the province of Toulouse. They resisted all attempts at conversion, and Pope Innocent launched a crusade from Lyons in 1209. After a siege of unprecedented length and savagery, the last heretic stronghold, the church of Montségur, capitulated, and the treaty of 1229 officially ended the war. However, the new bishop of Albi, Bernard de Castanet, continued to persecute suspected heretics, incurring the hatred of townsfolk and church canons alike. Mindful of continuing political unrest and the threat of popular uprising, de Castanet in 1282 began to rebuild the church of Albi.

The castlelike Gothic church of St. Cecile affords no foothold for assailants. Only the south porch, added two hundred years later, relieves its redoubtable façade. Preserved within is an intricately carved sixteenth-century *jubé,* or choir screen. It is so vividly detailed that Cardinal Richelieu, on a visit there, climbed a ladder and rapped the screen to convince himself it was made of stone. Renaissance artists brought in by Louis II decorated the walls and vaults of the sanctuary with handsome frescoes. The *jubé,* the murals, the south porch, all products of happier times, stand in sharp contrast to the military character of the church, a reminder of the terror that led to construction of this unique monument.

59

Vaulted nave. Above: Angel on choir screen.

Flamboyant Gothic south porch. *Thick, castlelike walls give Albi its military character.*

15th-century fortified gate and turret.

In a letter dated August 17, 1790, George Washington, who had been feted at Touro, wrote the congregation of this oldest *Touro Synagogue* surviving synagogue in North America: "May the children of Abraham who dwell in this land continue to merit and enjoy the good will of the other inhabitants, while everyone shall sit in safety under his own vine and fig tree, and there shall be none to make him afraid." He was addressing a handful of Jewish families whose roots in the New World went back to their expulsion from Spain and Portugal in 1492–97. A number of Jews who had fled the Inquisition and settled in Dutch-occupied East Brazil arrived at Newport, Rhode Island, in 1654, attracted by the state's doctrine of religious freedom.

Their perfect little Georgian building, dedicated in 1763, was designed by Peter Harrison, by vocation a merchant and sea captain. Touro has classically simple lines. Its Palladian windows and its forthright portico with Ionic columns enclosing the one doorway reveal Harrison's work at its harmonious best. Within, governed by Sephardic convention and advised in ritual needs by Rabbi Isaac Touro, recently arrived from Amsterdam, Harrison devised a galleried hall derived from the great *esnoga* in Amsterdam, the "mother synagogue" of European Sephardim. The bimah was centrally placed before the Ark, and the Ark itself was set against the east wall, so that worshipers facing it faced Jerusalem.

During the War of Independence the congregation fled Newport and the synagogue fell into disuse. In the 1780's it briefly became a hall for state assembly sessions. Later restored, Touro was made a national historic monument in 1946.

63

Bimah faces Ark in east wall. Above: Gateway and portico.

St. Peter's, the mightiest church in Christendom and the triumph of many talents, soars 428 feet above the Vatican Hill. It

Basilica of St. Peter

is the shrine of the first bishop of Rome, St. Peter, the "rock" upon which, Catholics believe, Christ built his church.

For more than 150 years it had been the dream of a succession of popes to build a new and more magnificent church worthy of Christ's vicar. Old St. Peter's, the basilica put up by Constantine in 324 over the apostle's tomb, was beyond repair, despite frequent attempts to shore it up. In 1503 Donato Bramante, commissioned by Pope Julius II, prepared the first design of any consequence. But in his lifetime only four massive piers and arches were raised. Over the next half-century plans of indifferent merit were offered, but not until the prodigious energy of Michelangelo was tapped in 1549 did the project near conclusion. Given unlimited authority by Pope Paul III, the Renaissance titan, then aged seventy-two, took up Bramante's central plan, with modifications, and work got under way.

The glory of the basilica is Michelangelo's stupendous dome, completed after his death, during the papacy of Sixtus V. The largest ever built in Europe after Rome's Pantheon, it is a double shell with a staircase between, where sightseers may mount to the viewer's gallery. Though Michelangelo had intended that the dome be visible from the piazza, the façade, also completed after his death and changed slightly from his design, unfortunately obscures the view. Giovanni Lorenzo Bernini completed the great complex by adding a fourfold colonnade (1656–67) enclosing an elliptical space that forms one of the world's monumental squares.

Aged Michelangelo's mighty dome. Above: His Pietà, *done when he was twenty-five.*

Left: Twisting columns of Bernini's baldacchino.

Glorious interior dome that soars above it.

Baroque Chair of St. Peter by Bernini.

The Ryoanji Garden in Kyoto is perhaps the most remarkable contemplative garden in all of Japan. Designed in 1499 by an

Ryoanji Temple

unknown Zen master, it consists of fifteen carefully chosen stones surrounded by sand, set out in formal groups of 5-2-3-2-3. Their placement is a matter of precedence and proportion, with the smaller or "weaker" stones subordinated to the larger or "stronger" ones. Except for the moss that clings to the bases of the stones, the garden is devoid of vegetation. It may not be entered and may be viewed only from the abbot's quarters. The purpose of the Zen garden is to create a tranquil, esthetically ordered setting where meditation might spark in the beholder an intuitive glimpse into the true nature of reality and man's oneness with the universe.

Zen Buddhism, a twelfth-century offshoot of classical Buddhism, stressed "truth" and "awareness" through direct, intuitive insight. Among its rituals is the arcane and mysterious tea ceremony, said to reflect Zen's ideals of harmony, purity, reverence, and tranquillity. Initiates must handle the vessels with precision, and attention is directed to the beauty of the utensils and the serenity of the surroundings. Even silence is part of the ceremony: the sound of water bubbling or a bird singing is meant to provide a respite from the temporal hubbub of the world outside.

The austerity of the Rinzai sect is reflected in the purity and formality of the rock garden. A Zen poem expressing the "way" to enlightenment says: "Sitting quietly doing nothing Spring comes and the grass grows by itself." In the solemn peace of the Ryoanji garden, a monk sits in meditation, awaiting *satori*, the lightninglike flash of insight into the unity of self and nature.

69

View of garden from abbot's quarters. Above: Water vessel.

A tranquil and ordered setting.

Similar esthetics govern tea ceremony.

Ceremony achieves serenity through ritual.

71

These churches, carved from stone monoliths on a rocky plateau in the mountains of northern Ethiopia, are unique in all

Lalibala

of religious architecture. Massive subterranean monuments, they are mainly basilican in form. Some have roofs that are level with the countryside, others are cut into the stone at different depths. Columns, moldings, and vaults are all hewn out of one block of tufa.

The churches were probably built around 1200 by the Ethiopian king Lalibala. According to legend, Lalibala's brother, the ruler at the time, heard it prophesied that Lalibala would take over the throne and tried to poison him. In a trance, the prince had a vision of an angel who commanded him to build churches out of the bowels of the earth. When Lalibala recovered, his brother abdicated, and the new king set out to fulfill God's command. In twenty-four years, twelve churches were built in the capital city of Roha, renamed Lalibala, on the southwest flank of the Abuna Yosef mountains.

There are two groups of churches, one on either side of the stream Yordanos, and a single church, Beta Giyorgis, set some distance apart. Best loved is Beta Maryam (the House of Mary), which stands 9.1 meters deep. It is the most ornamented of all the churches, from its chiseled relief cross on the roof to the New Testament frescoes within. Beta Giyorgis (the House of St. George), built after the others were completed, is dedicated to Ethiopia's patron saint. A huge monolith in the form of a sculptured cross, it is considered by many the most beautiful of all the rock churches.

73

Monolithic Beta Giyorgis. Above: Ancient crown at Axum.

Left: Beta Maryam—House of Mary—hewn from tufa rock.

Ethiopian Copts celebrate Christmas.

The first French settlers came to the island of Montréal, Canada, in 1642, intending to establish a Christian outpost *Notre Dame* among the Indians that would be a "veritable kingdom of God." The town of Ville-Marie de Montréal was founded some years later. Within its palisades churches went up, each one rapidly outgrown by its increasing congregation. In the early nineteenth century many of the faithful had to stand outside the old church of Notre Dame, built in 1672, to share in the celebration of mass held within.

The church that replaced it in the late nineteenth century was, in its time, the largest on the continent north of Mexico City. Designed by James O'Donnell, it seats 8,000 to 9,000 people, and its architectural elegance and sumptuous decor reflect the city's growing affluence. The Neo-Gothic façade is 136 feet wide and 213 feet high, with square towers separated by a parapet. In the west tower is North America's second largest bell, "Le Gros Bourdon," weighing 24,780 pounds. The overall impression of the interior is one of a vast theater dominated by a huge, illuminated altar screen set on a stagelike sanctuary. The predominantly blue vault is decorated with a gold fleur-de-lis pattern. Natural light, let in through four skylights, accents the florid decor.

When the building's foundation stone was put in place in 1824, the ecstatic crowd, according to a local newspaper, set the architect on it and gave him "an ovation greater than [had ever been given] his late colleague, Michelangelo." On his death in 1830, O'Donnell was buried in the crypt, a spot marked by a marble plaque, the only grave in the church to be so distinguished.

Skylight over organ. Above: Towers and parapet define cathedral.

Right: Vast interior seats up to 9,000 people.

Beautifully elaborate pulpit.

"I have no family, nor obligations; I have left my clients, I have refused commissions; I wish nothing but it. . . . What I am doing is my duty, nothing more, and I must do it." With that Antonio Gaudí gave up the world of architecture and retired to his workshop at the Sagrada Familia to devote his remaining time to it. His association with the church began in 1883; at the age of thirty-one he replaced Francisco de Paula del Villar, a highly respected but conventional architect who had left in a dispute with Sagrada's patrons.

Sagrada Familia

In his earlier years Gaudí completed some of the most startling buildings ever conceived. Paradoxically, for all his fantastic effects, he was obsessed with reality, using real people as models for his biblical characters. Like Rembrandt, he searched the city for suitable models. Searching for a donkey for the Flight from Egypt group, Gaudí said that people brought him "the finest donkeys in Barcelona," but he wanted "a poor, old, and weary donkey." He found it at last, pulling a cart owned by an old and weary woman. In order to take plaster casts of the animal it had to be hoisted in the air. The owner, he said, "wept throughout for fear that her beast would not escape with its life."

At the age of sixty-two, this Catalan genius moved into his studio at the Sagrada, the one-time dandy lionized by the well-to-do now living like an indigent. In June, 1926, while on his way to services at the church of San Felipe Neri, he was struck by a trolley car. His funeral cortege wound nearly a mile to Barcelona cathedral, then to the Sagrada Familia, where he was buried in the crypt. He lies in the unfinished monument by special dispensation.

81

Unique façade is Gaudí's masterpiece. Above: Decorative detail in mosaic.

St. James's church in Sydney is one of the earliest examples of Colonial Georgian architecture in Australia. Basically a simplified version of the sophisticated style that flourished in eighteenth-century England, Colonial Georgian had a grace and charm that entirely suited the development of the colony.

St. James's Church

Australia was settled along the eastern seaboard mainly by convicts exiled from England. When Lachlan Macquarie became first governor of Sydney in 1813, he dreamed of transforming the frontier settlement into a thriving city. Francis Greenaway, a former architect who had been convicted of forgery, helped Governor Macquarie realize his dream. Greenaway was described as "the most sensitive and talented architect in Australia's history."

Designed as a simple rectangular building, St. James's has classical porticoes on each long side of the church, round arched windows and a square tower at the west end, and a copper-covered, 170-foot spire. Because it was too expensive to import high-quality building materials from Europe, the church was built largely of local inferior sandstone bricks. The interior is decorated with memorials to Australia's first settlers and the explorers who opened up the new continent.

By colonial standards, St. James's was considered a sophisticated church. Situated in the center of town, it attracted the first aristocrats and upper-class families to its Sunday services. Built during the "golden age" of Australian architecture, which flourished from 1788–1840, St. James's exemplifies the Colonial Georgian style of architecture and reflects the beginnings of Australian culture.

83

Copper-covered spire rises above Colonial Georgian façade. Above: Pristine interior.

During the blitz, Winston Churchill said, "St. Paul's is London," and indeed it was a symbol of the spirit that helped see Londoners through the dark hours of World War II. Though it suffered incendiary attacks and two damaging hits by the Luftwaffe, the church survived, and at war's end the dome of St. Paul's still dominated the city as it had for 250 years.

St. Paul's Cathedral

London's cathedral looms over Ludgate Hill, the legendary site of a Roman temple. Here stood London's great medieval cathedral, affectionately known as Old St. Paul's, until it was ravaged by the Great Fire of 1666. After several attempts at repair, it was decided that a new church should be built by Christopher Wren.

The glory of St. Paul's, England's only classical cathedral, is its dome. London's cathedral, Wren knew, had to have a towering central element, a reflection of civic pride and power. To achieve this great height, he ingeniously constructed a double dome. Between the two he set a tall brick cone on which the lantern rests. At the crossing, the inner dome rises 100 feet to an encircling tier of windows where, the story goes, Sir Christopher had himself hauled up in a basket to supervise construction. Just below it is the "whispering gallery," where acoustics are so acute that at any point a whisper can be heard on the opposite side, 107 feet away.

In his final years, Wren often visited the cathedral to admire his work. At the age of ninety-one, in 1723, he made such a visit on a particularly chilly February day, and he died soon after. He was buried in the crypt. On his tomb is this inscription in Latin: *Si monumentum requiris, circumspice*—"If you would find his monument, look around you."

85

Christopher Wren's majestic dome crowns classical exterior. Above: View of bell tower.

View of nave, looking east.

Spiral and fluted columns surround high altar.

Cathedral of Santa Maria

Burgos Cathedral

Built into a hillside on many levels, Burgos, erected along French lines, is Spain's first great Gothic cathedral. It owes its origin to founder-bishop Mauricio, who, stirred by the sight of the great Île-de-France cathedrals, determined to build himself a new church. In July, 1221, it was begun.

Typically Gothic are the cathedral's sculptured portals. Over the Puerta del Sarmental on the south side is the first major Gothic sculpture in Spain—the figure of an Apocalyptic Christ and the Evangelists. The façade is composed of traditional elements—triple portal, rose window, and twin towers—but the openwork spires are German, done by Hans of Colonia, who moved to Spain in 1442 and, with his son and grandson, dominated the cathedral works for three generations.

Spotlighted in a chapel all to itself hangs the "Christ of Burgos," a life-size wooden figure with movable arms and legs, buffalo-hide skin, a wig of real hair, and a red Castilian petticoat. The figure has long been an object of awed devotion, and peasants in earlier times believed that the nails and hair of the image grew. Within the dark choir is the stone that covers the dust of El Cid and his wife Ximena. His coffer, hung on the wall of the sacristy, is one of the most popular objects in the church. According to legend, when he was pressed for cash he pledged his coffer, purportedly filled with gold though in reality with sand, to credulous Jewish moneylenders. It is said, however, that he redeemed the pledge. The Cid's bones, stolen during the Peninsular War, were discovered after some search in western Germany. They were returned and finally laid to rest in Burgos in 1921.

Lacy spires rise above village's red-tiled roofs. Above: Sculptural detail from Capilla del Condestable.

Left: Cathedral courtyard.

Christ and evangelists over Puerta del Sarmental.

Exterior sculptures.

91

Vienna had been Europe's eastern outpost, standing against the hordes sweeping out of the Eurasian heartland ever since Rome *St. Stephen's Cathedral* first camped its legions on the Danube. When the twelfth-century Romanesque church went up where St. Stephen's now stands, Vienna was still a frontier town. With traffic brought in by the Crusades, however, the city soon became a mediator and an avenue of commerce with the East. It was in Vienna that Richard the Lion-Hearted, returning from the Crusades, was captured. His enormous ransom was spent to enlarge the city's fortified walls. In this medieval city, St. Stephen's old church was gradually transformed into Vienna's enduring symbol and Austria's best-known Gothic church.

A typical hall church, St. Stephen's was enlarged about 1358 under the sponsorship of Rudolf IV, the most precocious of the Hapsburgs. Although construction took some two hundred years, St. Stephen's basically followed the plan of Rudolf and his architect, Meister Wenzla of Klosterneuberg. The intimate connection between the Hapsburgs and the church is celebrated in several fourteenth-century windows of the Ducal Chapel, as well as in numerous life-size figures, clad in fashionable fifteenth-century dress, studding the façade. Duke Albrecht II, on the south tower, is singled out as a brilliant psychological portrait. The "Servant's Madonna" an evocative statue inside the church, is a particular favorite. Legend tells us that when a maid falsely accused of theft prayed to the figure, she was told that the Virgin paid no heed to servants. Nonetheless, she was found innocent, and her penitent mistress donated the statue to St. Stephen's.

93

Brilliantly patterned roof was restored after World War II bombing.

Left: Ablaze with light during high mass.

Magnificent two-tiered triptych.

Stoning of St. Stephen, by Messerschmidt.

Candlelight in a side chapel.

95

Abbey and Cathedral Church of the Assumption

Monreale Cathedral

When the Normans invaded Sicily in 1061, freeing it from the Saracens, they immediately began to put up churches that stand today as testimony to their building skill, initiative, and energy. Most notable are the three great cathedrals of Cefalu, Palermo, and Monreale, all built between 1130 and 1200 and all mingling successive styles and cultures.

Monreale, which was founded by William II ("the Good") in 1174 on a hill overlooking Palermo, is a typical mixture of styles: twin Norman towers, interlaced and pointed arches of Islamic heritage, and an interior covered with Byzantine mosaics that tell Old and New Testament stories. The majestic bronze doors, the largest of their time, are original twelfth-century castings by the sculptor Bonanno of Pisa. Decorated with forty-two sculptured panels illustrating biblical scenes, these portals are similar in character to the great doors he later constructed for the *duomo* at Pisa. Adjoining the cathedral are the remains of Monreale's twelfth-century cloisters, with Arabic pointed arches and sumptuously decorated paired marble columns, alternately plain, multicolored, and ornately encrusted with mosaics and intricately carved designs.

Buried at Monreale are many of the Norman kings who built Sicily's great cathedrals, among them William himself, whose sarcophagus lies in the chapel to the right of the choir. St. Louis—Louis IX of France—was interred at Monreale after he died in Tunis while leading the Eighth Crusade. Although his body was removed to the abbey church of St. Denis in Paris, in 1278 his heart and intestines were enshrined as holy relics at Monreale.

Norman towers blend with Islamic arches. Above: Cloisters.

Right: Inside, Islam blends with Byzantine mosaics.

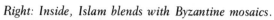

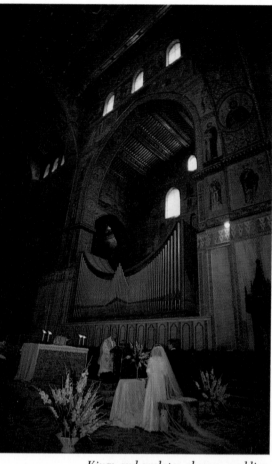

Mosaics of apse.

Kings and prelates observe wedding.

Sculptured panels of side chapel.

The Pilgrimage Church of Die Wies reflects the Baroque style that spread northward from Italy after the Renaissance and *Die Wies*

found its apogee in the churches and palaces of southern Germany and Austria in the eighteenth century. It was built in 1745 to house a statue of the "Flagellated Savior," made by two monks from the monastery of Steingaden. Painted in garish colors, the wooden statue was carried through the streets every Good Friday. The villagers grew so terrified of the macabre statue that in 1734 it was hidden away in an attic. Four years later, it was moved to a farm at Die Wies. During evening prayers on June 14, 1738, it was reported that tears appeared in the eyes of the statue. News of this miracle spread quickly, and Die Wies soon became a popular pilgrimage goal. When a chapel became too small to hold the pilgrims, a new and larger church was built.

Die Wies was designed by Dominikus Zimmermann, who had already gained fame as the architect of a pilgrimage church at Steinhausen. Though the exterior is unassuming, there are Baroque splendors within. The interior plan, basically a longitudinal oval, is of minimal importance in relation to the theatrical effect created by the profusion of stucco, gilding, and colorful *scagliola* (imitation marble) decoration. The shallow wooden vault is covered by an enormous fresco that creates the illusion of a dome. The pulpit is an elaborate structure displaying innumerable cherubs amidst the Pentecostal storm that accompanies the presence of the Holy Spirit. In contrast to such opulence, the figure of the Flagellated Savior in the sanctuary remains as macabre today as it was at the outset of its miraculous saga.

Simple exterior houses Baroque splendor. Above: Sundial.

Ceiling art gives illusion of height.   *Sanctuary houses statue of "Flagellated Savior."*

Curlicues surround organ loft.

By the mid-nineteenth century, synagogue architecture had adapted the Moorish style, which the Jews felt best reflected their ancient heritage. The outstanding example of a Moorish Revival synagogue is the nineteenth-century synagogue in Florence, Italy. It owes its existence to David Levi, president of the Council of the Florence Jewish Community, who willed his entire estate to fund the building of a "monumental temple worthy of Florence." The architects included Mariano Falcini, Vincenzo Micheli, and Mauro Treves, one of the earliest Jewish architects to emerge in the nineteenth century.

Florence Synagogue

The exterior consists of typically Moorish horseshoe-shaped arches, a central dome that rises majestically above the crossing, and twin minaret "staircase" towers with bulbous cupolas in the Byzantine manner. The elaborate interior is an unbroken expanse of tile, mosaic, and glass, covered with Spanish-Moorish patterns derived from the fourteenth-century synagogue of Toledo, Spain. Ornately carved and decorated wood, intricately worked bronze, and polychromed tiles, combined with the multiple lights of standing candelabra and wall sconces, created a setting of Byzantine splendor and Moorish opulence. The Ark stands raised in an enclosed area before the central reading platform.

Florence's synagogue suffered grave injury during the flood of the Arno in 1966. Water reached a height of six feet within the synagogue, damaging 90 of the 120 ancient Torah scrolls, as well as some 15,000 books in the congregation's library. A massive effort by world Jewry has since restored much of the great structure to its original condition.

Intricately detailed Ark. Above: Moorish façade and dome.

The mission church of San Esteban del Rey crowns a rugged New Mexico mesa, 350 feet above the surrounding

San Esteban del Rey

desert. Site of an ancient pueblo, "sky-crowned Acoma" was home for the Acoma Indians, who for centuries had hauled food and fuel up a torturous trail broken intermittently by steps and ladders to their eagle's-nest abode. Visited in 1564 by Coronado, the pueblo was razed by the Spaniards in retaliation for an Indian attack in 1598, then was rebuilt by them. When the Spaniards left, Acoma was abandoned. In 1629 the Franciscan friar Juan Ramirez arrived alone and on foot, having walked from Santa Fe to found a mission atop the pueblo in the sky.

New Mexico's mission churches are unique in Spanish colonial architecture. Their distinction lies in a near-perfect blend of Spanish and Indian influences. Acoma, the exemplary New Mexico mission church, is basically Spanish in plan, but the construction and ornamental detail are traditionally Indian. The job of building the church, which took about thirteen years, must have been literally backbreaking. All materials—wood, water to mix the clay for adobe bricks, even soil for the burial ground—were carried laboriously on the backs of the Indians up incredibly steep trails. It is said that the enormous vigas, or roof beams were cut and dressed from felled trees and then dragged here from the San Mateo mountains some thirty miles away. The raw mix for the adobe brick was kneaded on top of the mesa by Indian women using their feet and hoes to work the clay. The men attended to the more skilled tasks, such as the raising of the roof beams, the carpentry, and the decorative carving and painting of the corbels, or roof-beam supports.

107

Adobe brick realizes Spanish design. Above: Hand-carved railing.

Pigeons and St. Mark's Piazza, and the great basilica of Venice rising over the setting like a caliph's dream, have fascinated

Basilica of St. Mark

tourists and pilgrims for centuries. Poets from Petrarch to Byron have written of it; Mark Twain sipped his coffee at a corner café. Under the bronze horses on the west façade of St. Mark's, stolen from Constantinople in the Fourth Crusade, the visitor stands bemused in a piazza Napoleon called the "grandest salon in Europe."

Built on pilings in a marshy lagoon to which its inhabitants fled in the fifth century from Attila, Venice became a maritime power and the great broker between East and West during the Middle Ages. As the city grew, its original patron saint, Theodore, was somehow dispossessed and soon after the theft of St. Mark's body from Alexandria, Egypt, around 829, the first basilica to the evangelist was raised. History tells us that two enterprising Venetian sea captains in Alexandria managed through a ruse to spirit away St. Mark's remains. When the theft was discovered, Moslems set out in pursuit, but turned back when they discovered that the Venetians had covered the body with hams, a meat prohibited to members of the Moslem faith.

St. Mark's has been called an "Oriental fantasy" without, and a "museum of Venetian acquisitiveness" inside. The beauty of St. Mark's cavernous interior lies in the unbroken expanse of multicolored marble and mosaics set against a gold background. In this dim interior the gem-encrusted Pala d'Oro, one of the most celebrated altar screens ever conceived, hides, near the high altar, a sarcophagus said to contain the remains of St. Mark. Many believe, however, that the body was destroyed by a fire after it had been brought from Egypt.

109

Venice's "Oriental fantasy." Above: World-famous bronze horses.

Cavernous interior: "A museum of Venetian acquisitiveness."

111

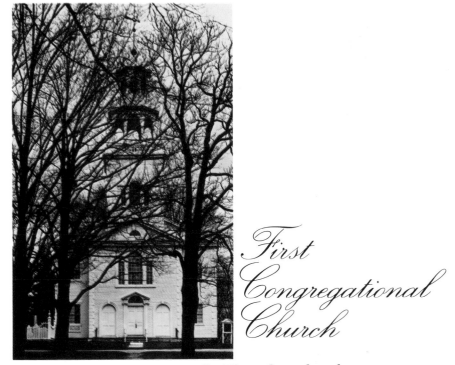

First
Congregational
Church

The early settlers who came to New England in search of religious freedom turned away not only from traditional English liturgy, but from traditional church architecture, as well. Their first churches, called "meeting houses," were boxlike affairs, completely unadorned. In time, as New Englanders left behind some of their Puritan militancy, traditional elements returned to church architecture.

During the Federal period, white-steepled churches began to reappear. The First Congregational Church of Bennington was designed and built in 1804–06 by Lavius Fillmore, who took for his model a plate from the first native handbook on architecture, Asher Benjamin's *Country Builder's Assistant*, published in 1787. But Bennington was not a copy. It was a creative adaptation by Fillmore, whose rounded door tops and upper windows and arcaded belfry reflect a grace note to the Federal style. Typical of the Federal style are the triple doors in front and the use of Palladian windows and classical ornamentation.

Altered extensively during the Victorian era, the building was meticulously restored in 1937. At the rear of the galleries were found pews with seven-foot sides, apparently a segregated area for blacks. In the gallery, unmarried men sat to one side and single women sat opposite. A great variety of carvings were found in the bachelors' pews: initials, animal designs, even a scriptural quote from Matthew. The women's gallery was pristine. Adjacent to the church is the old cemetery, where the heroes of the Battle of Bennington lie. The poet Robert Frost is buried here, too, in a setting that still retains the simplicity of a bygone era.

113

Graceful double pulpit. Above: Triple-tiered tower is typical of New England Federal churches.

Centuries of island life have shaped the architecture of the Greek Cyclades, a group of thirtynine islands in the Aegean

Village Church

Sea surrounding the sacred Isle of Delos, one of the most important religious sites of ancient Greece. Here the goddess Leto is said to have taken refuge from Hera, jealous wife of Zeus, the chief Olympian deity, in order to give birth to the twins Apollo and Artemis, children of Zeus himself. Today Delos is no longer inhabited. Its gods and people have long since fled, and its serenity and ancient ruins attract only tourists. But the island's stones did not go to waste. Stripped by the Venetians of most of its stone and marble for their palaces and churches in the Middle Ages, it became a quarry as well for the villagers of neighboring Mykonos. Constantly threatened by pirates and marauding Turks, the beleaguered islanders vowed, if spared, to raise yet another church in the hope of maintaining God's favor.

There are hundreds of churches on tiny, sun-scorched, treeless Mykonos—some say one for each day of the year. Generally they are similar in shape to the houses, for the most part differing only in their roofs. The flat-roofed church with a "dome" or terrace is the most primitive and the favorite among the islanders. Mostly, however, the vaulted church is seen. The stark exteriors are all whitewashed; the only colors permitted by tradition are pink or blue on the domes or roofs of the churches. Whitewashing of exteriors is a relatively recent custom. Only after the revolution against the Turks in 1821 could the Greek islanders relax. Until then, fear of pirates made inconspicuousness a lifesaving necessity, and homes and churches were kept dark, hidden away among the rocks.

Bright, whitewashed exteriors are characteristic of Mykonos's hundreds of churches.

The Golden Temple in the city of Amritsar in the hilly northwestern Punjab is the most sacred shrine of the Sikhs.

Golden Temple

Founded by Ram Das, the Sikhs' fourth guru, or teacher, the temple was built on land granted them by the Mogul emperor Akbar. Persecuted later by less tolerant Moguls, then battered by Islamic Afghans as the Mogul rule declined, the Sikhs struggled for supremacy in the Punjab throughout the eighteenth century. In the battles with the marauding Afghans, the temple at Amritsar was periodically attacked and defiled. Eventually the Afghans were defeated and the victorious Sikhs triumphantly rebuilt their temple.

The Harimandir, or main temple, which rises from an island in the center of a sacred pool, is connected to land by a 200-foot marble causeway. Eclectic in design, it shows Mogul influence in the use of marble inlaid with semiprecious stones: lapis lazuli, onyx, carnelian, and mother-of-pearl. The gilded surface is covered with verses from the Granth Sahib, the Sikhs' holy book. A pavilion in the center of the roof, the Shish Mahal or Mirror Room, is held in veneration because it is believed that Govind Singh, the tenth and last guru, spent many hours here.

The Granth Sahib, a compilation of writings of Sikh, Hindu, and Moslem holy men, rests on a divan in a special room within the temple. Pilgrims throw offerings of money or flowers onto a sheet spread in the middle of the room, then join in the chanting of scripture. When the holy book is not being read, it is reverently brushed by an attendant with a fly-whisk made of yak's hair, an ancient symbol of royalty.

117

Harimandir rests on island in pool. Above: Temple guardian.

Upper story of literally Golden Temple.

Causeway over pool to temple.   *Pigeons roost among gilded domes.*

Reading from Granth Sahib—holy writ.

Turbaned Sikhs in courtyard.

Cloth is spread to receive offerings.

119

The cathedral of Pisa was begun in 1067 to commemorate the Pisans' rout of the Saracens from Sicily. Constructed almost *Pisa Cathedral* entirely of dazzling white marble, it was designed by an architect named Buschetto, about whom little is known. Basically basilican in plan, the church is in the form of a Latin cross. Suspended at the crossing is a beautiful bronze lamp encircled by cherubs, affectionately known as "Galileo's Lamp." The scientist allegedly discovered the principle of the pendulum as he watched the lamp swinging. The circular baptistery contains one of the sculptural masterworks of the Middle Ages, the pulpit by Nicola Pisano, completed in 1266. Resting on richly colored stone and marble columns, the pulpit is decorated with carved relief panels depicting episodes from the Nativity, the Purification, the Adoration of the Magi, the Crucifixion, and the Last Judgment.

Undoubtedly the most famous building in the complex is the campanile—the Leaning Tower of Pisa. The building began to settle to one side before it was half finished by the noted sculptor and architect Bonanno Pisano, who abandoned the project about midway. Subsequent architects completed the structure, but their attempts to correct its list were unsuccessful. The 184-foot tower was already sixteen feet out of plumb in the 1700's, and it continued to shift even into the twentieth century. Concrete, recently poured into and around the towered base seems to have halted, at least temporarily, the continuing slide. Here Galileo conducted his famous experiments, dropping weights from the tower's top in order to determine the laws relating to the velocity of falling objects.

121

Latin cross of duomo *points to baptistery. Above: Leaning Tower.*

In 1573, during the reign of Philip II of Spain, the first church of Mexico, christened the Metropolitan Church by Pope Paul

Mexico City Cathedral

III, was pulled down to make way for a more magnificent structure. Mexico City's massive cathedral of basalt and buff-colored sandstone is probably the largest church in the Americas. Its weathered façade is topped by two towers with bell-shaped domes. In the west tower is the 27,000-pound bell, called Santa Maria de Guadalupe, reputedly the continent's biggest. Although the façade is adorned with typical Baroque ornaments—elaborate bas-reliefs, cornices, statues, and gargoyles—the cathedral looks almost austere when contrasted with the adjoining Sagrario, a small church where consecrated furnishings are stored.

In the Capilla de los Reyes, one of the chapels girdling the interior of the cathedral, stands the Altar of the Kings. Carved entirely of wood and covered with gold leaf, it is a maze of niches, paintings, and pilasters. Another altarpiece, the most popular in the cathedral, is the Altar of Pardon. The painting set into the bottom, a Madonna and Child, is said to be the work of a Flemish painter named Pereyns. Pereyns purportedly was accused of heresy because he refused to paint sacred subjects, and he was required to paint this scene on the door of his jail cell. Another popular image is El Señor de Cacao ("Our Lord of the Cacao Beans"), in St. Joseph's Chapel. It is said that the ancient figure stood outside the first cathedral, soliciting alms for the new construction. Indians who were too poor to give coins dropped cacao beans in the plate. The gem of the cathedral is *The Virgin of Bethlehem* by Murillo, now in La Pequeña Capilla del Cabildo, a small chapel off the sacristy.

123

Brightly lit façade at night. Above: Cardinal presides over Holy Week mass.

Dramatic view of North America's largest church.

Holy Thursday service. Procession during Easter services.

124

Priests at prayer.

Abbey Church of St. Mary Magdalen

The church of La Madeleine at Vézelay stands at the summit of a hill in the province of Burgundy in southeastern France. To-

La Madeleine

day Vézelay is a sleepy country town, but nearly a thousand years ago pilgrims flocked to worship at the shrine of Mary Magdalen, whose remains were reputedly found in the church's ninth-century crypt. In time, Vézelay became the starting point for one of the great pilgrimage routes across France. Soon the old church was so crowded that the Cluniac abbot, Artaud, decided to rebuild it on a larger scale. Despite a series of bizarre and violent events, including a fire on the eve of Mary Magdalen's feast day in 1120, in which more than a thousand worshipers perished, the church was finally completed in 1206.

La Madeleine's chief glory is its narthex, or porch, with its sculptured portals, where pilgrims gathered for the processions down the aisles. In the tympanum above the central opening is a splendid portrayal of Christ in Majesty with the apostles seated beneath his outstretched arms. The world's afflicted, to whom the gospel will be carried, are shown on the lintel below.

Toward the end of the thirteenth century other relics of Mary Magdalen were found at the abbey of St. Maximum in Provence, and Vézelay became a neglected backwater. Its decaying relics were dispersed in the Huguenot rebellion of 1569. La Madeleine was saved in the nineteenth century, when its merit as a Romanesque monument was publicized by the writer Prosper Mérimée. Today, fully restored, it stands as a reminder of a time of faith when thousands traveled across France to share the presence of a saint's bones.

127

Great porch. Above: Medieval vintners surmount interior column.

Glimpse of nave through portals of narthex.

Chevet and crossing tower.

The dream of Edward the Confessor, king of England from 1044 to 1066, was to build a monastery on an island in the River *Westminster Abbey*

Thames called Westminster Eyot, but only the abbey church was completed in his lifetime. Construction of the great Westminster Abbey, now a near neighbor of London's Houses of Parliament, was largely the work of Henry III, who lavished unimaginable sums on it before being forced to stop work in 1269 for lack of funds. Although English Gothic was moving in a different direction, Henry, an ardent francophile, chose French Gothic, then at the peak of its fame, as his model. Henry's dream was not only for a great coronation church but also for a burial place for himself and his successors. To that end he chose the best materials and finest craftsmen. Work rolls list as many as 800 men employed at one time in 1250.

Although much of the church was completed in Henry's lifetime, it took the monks two and a half centuries of alms-gathering, even with the aid of an occasional benefactor, to finish the nave. A later addition to the abbey was the chapel of Henry VII, built during England's glorious phase of late Perpendicular Gothic.

Westminster has been England's coronation church since the Norman Conquest. The oak coronation chair was built by Edward I in 1300 to enclose the ancient Stone of Scone, upon which Scottish kings sat to be crowned and won by Edward in 1296. Buried in Westminster are England's illustrious dead: Henry V, the victor of Agincourt; Queen Elizabeth; and Mary Queen of Scots. In the Poets' Corner lie Chaucer, Tennyson, Browning, and T. S. Eliot, and around the tomb of Sir Isaac Newton have been gathered the ashes of other great scientists.

131

Celebration of the abbey's 900th anniversary. Above: Union Jack waves above soaring tower.

Order of Bath service.   *Henry VII's Chapel facing east (above) and west (right).*

Tomb of Edward the Confessor.

132

The soaring triangle of Elkins Park Synagogue in a suburb of Philadelphia, Pennsylvania, symbolically embodies one of Judaism's most revered settings: Mount Sinai, the height on which God gave Moses the tablets of the law. When the Elkins Park congregation Beth Sholom first organized in 1917, the movement toward Reform Judaism, begun earlier in Germany, had already taken root in the United States. As this reform spirit broke with tradition by placing increased emphasis on the sermon, a simplified service, and mixed seating of men and women, Judaism moved away from traditional design toward the unconventional in synagogue construction. Intrigued by an idea broached by the rabbi of Beth Sholom, Frank Lloyd Wright, perhaps America's most radical architect, agreed in 1953 to design a new synagogue for Elkins Park.

Beth Sholom
Synagogue

Sheathed in white glass panels with a cream-colored plastic skin within, the new building becomes literally a "mountain of light." Covering an immense tripod of steel beams, the synagogue rises 100 feet to its apex. Each of the three ridged sides is studded with seven lights, representing Judaism's classical symbol, the seven-branched menorah. Using the triangle as his module, Wright unified inner space in this "hosanna to the living god." Seated in an amphitheater, 1,100 worshipers face one another around the bimah, while on the wall before them is suspended the central element of the synagogue, the Ark, enclosed at Elkins Park within an immense prism, forty feet of wooden monolith lighted from within.

In a letter of praise to the architect, Beth Sholom's rabbi wrote, "You have incarnated my 'inspired thought' in steel and glass and concrete and copper."

Wright's "mountain of light." Above: Interior shows white glass panels.

On a wall within the sanctuary of San Vitale, a mosaic shows Justinian standing with his imperial court. It is one of the

San Vitale

world's famous portraits. Ravenna, which fell to the Ostrogoths in 493, was retaken by Justinian in 540. Under Justinian, Ravenna entered a golden age of church-building, but the city was forgotten after the Western Empire fell in the eighth century, and for more than 1,200 years it remained a historical backwater. Today it is treasured for its architecture and mosaics, with the greatest number of surviving Byzantine churches in the West. San Vitale is the most interesting of these. It is octagonal in shape, with a central space surrounded by an aisle and galleries above. A dome, supported by arches, is built of clay pots fitted ingeniously into each other, and is protected by a timbered roof over which tile has been laid.

 Inside the church, muted light enters through eight windows in the drum from which the dome rises over its eight supporting piers. Although the dome is decorated with eighteenth-century frescoes, and some marble veneer is gone, the remaining fabric, walls, arches, and especially the sanctuary, are an unbroken expanse of marble and glittering mosaics. The Romans had long used mosaics, but theirs were of stone. The Ravenna mosaics are made of glass, intricately fused cubes on which gold leaf or pigments were laid and then covered with a thin glass film. These gleaming "tesserae," as the cubes were called, create the shifting color and light that is the chief delight of San Vitale. Within the sanctuary are the well-known imperial portraits: Justinian, wearing the royal purple, offers a golden bowl to the church, while opposite, his empress, Theodora, brings a chalice as a gift.

137

Octagonal shape is Byzantine. Above: Emperor Justinian.

Left: Gleaming "tesserae" mosaics are glory of Ravenna.

Theodora offers chalice to church.

Capital supports 5th-century arches.

Great Church of the Holy Wisdom

Hagia Sophia

When the armies of Belisarius entered Rome in 536 and later Ravenna, the emperor Justinian united the eastern and western halves of the Roman Empire. Following the tradition of conquerors, he built a number of great public buildings to celebrate his victories, including the Church of the Holy Wisdom—Hagia Sophia—in Constantinople, today's Istanbul.

The dominant feature of Hagia Sophia is its enormous dome. Justinian selected as his architects two master mathematicians, Anthemius of Tralles and Isidorus of Miletus, but they had little experience in enclosing so huge a volume of space in a domed structure. Their invention, a triangular unit of vaulting known as the pendentive, enabled them to place the huge saucer-shaped dome on a square base, revolutionizing architecture throughout the Byzantine world.

In order to raise a church as quickly as possible, Justinian gathered about him "all the artisans of the world." Some say there were 100 foremen, each with 100 workers under him. Nearly seven years later, on December 27, 537, Hagia Sophia was completed. The church's interior was a glittering expanse of marble and mosaic. Most of the figured mosaic work was destroyed in 1453, when Constantinople was overrun by the Turks, who sacked the city and transformed the church into a mosque. In the 1930's, under the Turkish president Kemal Ataturk, Hagia Sophia became a museum, and restoration of the interior mosaics was begun. Much of the interior has faded and the marble has lost its light and polish. Despite the accumulation of centuries of disfiguring coats of plaster, the monument remains one of the world's marvels of engineering and of enclosed space.

141

Tiers of columns and windows flank the nave. Above: Acanthus-leaf pattern adorns capital.

Enormous dome, set on pendentives, dominates this masterpiece of Byzantine architecture.

Vierzehnheiligen was erected in 1735 to commemorate a shepherd's vision of the Christ Child with fourteen children,

Vierzehnheiligen

the *Nothelfer* or Helper Saints. It sits on a hill overlooking the River Main in Franconia, Germany. From the first appearance of the vision in 1445, a small chapel put up on the site attracted many pilgrims. In time, the abbot of Langheim and the bishop of Bamberg decided to replace the chapel with a larger church.

Balthasar Neumann, Germany's foremost Baroque architect, designed an interior with an ingenious arrangement of ovals and circles, ribs and domes, which created brilliant spatial effects. The focus is the Shrine of the Fourteen Helper Saints, centrally located under the huge longitudinal oval of the nave. An audacious fantasy, unrivaled in any eighteenth-century church, the ornate freestanding structure was designed by Jacob Michael Küchel after Neumann's death and remains one of the extraordinary Rococo masterpieces. The shrine is part *baldacchino*, and is sometimes compared to the upper part of a state coach. At each corner of an encircling balustrade are life-size figures of the saints; the top is crowned by a sunburst from which emerge four figures of the Christ child. Rococo scrolls surround the base of the shrine on which are seated white and gold figures made of *scagliola*, a hard plaster that can be worked to a very fine polish. Another Rococo masterpiece is Küchel's pulpit, which depicts the theme of divine inspiration as a magnificent sunburst. Carved in relief on the body of the pulpit are the four evangelists shown spreading the Word to the four continents, which are represented by heads of *putti*—infant angels—peering out amidst the sunburst.

145

Fantastic shrine of Fourteen Helper Saints. Above: Façade.

One of the world's more startling ecclesiastical buildings is Oscar Niemeyer's cathedral of Brasilia, a church fashioned

Brasilia Cathedral

out of sixteen hollow concrete ribs curving upward from a 200-foot cement circle to a 40-foot roof, 100 feet above the ground. Against the flat sweep of the immense surrounding plaza, it gathers itself up like a vast sculptural symbol of Christ's sacrifice, the Crown of Thorns.

The use of reinforced concrete, with its "infinite possibilities," allowed Niemeyer to envision a structure "that would be a monumental piece of sculpture, embodying a religious idea." The old cathedrals, he noted, "were richly decorated façades and interiors. I wanted to create an architecture no longer dependent on traditional symbols with two façades, but rather one structure, a simple, uniform work, a piece of art."

Brasilia's interior is simply a very large open space, seating 4,000, that rises in one unbroken expanse to the delicate cross at the top. Traditional divisions into chancel, nave, and porch no longer exist. The altar platform, the choir loft, the pulpit, and seating units are all freestanding structures within the circular ground plan. This provides an unobstructed area around the perimeter which is used for processions on festival days. It allows even those farthest away to be near enough to see and hear clearly, and to participate in celebrating the mass. Around the perimeter, thirteen small chapels are used for private services.

Completed in 1973, Brasilia represents a journey from the anonymous creators of the cathedrals of the past to the personal statement of the moderns.

147

Cathedral ribs symbolize Crown of Thorns. Scale (above) is vast.

Cathedral of Notre Dame

One of the sublime views in France is the sight, on the road from Paris to Chartres, of the oddly disparate spires rising above *Chartres*

the horizon out of the wheat fields of the Beauce. The south spire, the elder, was built about 1160. The late Gothic north tower came 350 years later. According to legend, Chartres had been a pagan shrine in Gallo-Roman times, then a site on which a succession of churches arose, drawing pilgrims to a sacred well which has recently been uncovered in the ninth-century crypt far below the high altar. Gradually the shrine was transformed to the cult of the Virgin. Twice razed by fire in a span of sixty years, Chartres was rebuilt by the extraordinary passion of donors, rich and poor alike, and especially the guilds, whose devotion is recorded in many of the cathedral's windows.

Stained glass has never been greater than at Chartres. In the Middle Ages light was considered "a divine essence," and as it passed through the colored glass, windows came alive. The most famous stained-glass windows of the Middle Ages appeared in the 1140's over the west doors, the Tree of Jesse at the right, scenes from the Life of Christ in the center, and the Passion of Christ at the left, above the Portail Royale. Of the original 186 windows, 172 great panels remain.

Chartres is an incomparable ensemble of sculpture, glass, and architecture. But it is probably in the cathedral's radiant interior that one comes closest to the emotional impact of the church, best expressed in the twelfth century by the Abbot Suger: "When one stands before the glorious colors from the sacred windows, it is as if the viewer were transported halfway to heaven."

149

Disparate spires are distinctive feature of façade. Above: New Testament figures at north portal.

Left: "Divine essence" floods interior through stained-glass windows.

Marriage ceremony at high altar.

11th-century Miracle window (left); detail of King Saul.

St. Patrick's Neo-Gothic cathedral in the city of Melbourne is for many the finest ecclesiastical building in Australia. Be-

St. Patricks' Cathedral

gun in the mid-nineteenth century, when Melbourne was still largely a pioneer town, its construction was brought to a halt by the discovery of gold, which sent many members of the work force rushing off to strike it rich. Gold and increased wealth brought in their wake not only a desire for buildings on a grander scale but also a rush of English-trained architects to help build thriving Melbourne.

Foremost among them was William Wardell, whose early training as an engineer stood him in good stead. Early in his career he had come under the influence of Augustus Pugin, the principal advocate of the Gothic Revival movement, and turned his attention to the study of medieval buildings. Commissions for over thirty churches came his way before he left England in 1858. On his arrival in Melbourne, the provincial government of Victoria snatched him up as its architect, allowing him the luxury of a private practice. His first commission was the reconstruction of St. Patrick's.

St. Patrick's is considered Wardell's masterpiece. Its east end, consisting of chapels radiating around a semicircular walkway, is highly regarded for the dramatic contrast between its native basaltic blue stone and the lighter-colored sandstone that outlines windows, the slate roof, and pinnacles studding the buttresses. Three spires, made of light-colored Hawkesbury River freestone, were added later. This impressive monument stands as one of the finest examples of the Neo-Gothic in Australia.

153

Native basaltic blue stone contrasts with sandstone outlines and accents.

Magnificently sited above its sea wall, Palma reveals its massive southern flank, a buttressed palisade spiked with pinna-

Palma Cathedral

cles and pierced only by narrow lancet windows, reflecting the military character of Catalan Gothic. Only the Mirador Portal on the south wall, an entryway begun in 1308 and richly carved in the late Gothic manner, relieves the martial character of the façade.

The interior is overwhelming. The nave is flanked by narrow aisles, each as high as the vault of any English cathedral. Typical of Catalan Gothic are the chapels set in the wall between the huge inner buttresses, encircling the nave like a necklace of small sanctuaries. An oculus, or round window, Islamic in inspiration and filled with brilliantly colored bits of glass, is set in the wall at the junction of choir and nave, casting a fiery glow over what would otherwise be a dim interior.

In the late nineteenth century, a movement was begun to repair many of Spain's historical buildings that had been damaged during Napoleon's Peninsular Wars of 1805–14. Antonio Gaudí, the exuberant Catalan genius, was commissioned to restore a number of medieval monuments, including Palma. The choir was moved from its traditional Spanish position in the nave to the east end, the high altar was pulled forward, and the great choir screens were relegated to the side wall. Unmindful of the past, Gaudí introduced a touch of Art Nouveau to the church, setting new lighting fixtures like spikey circlets fixed to piers around the nave. Above the altar he hung an immense metal chandelier, which in its medieval setting offends some, delights others, and reaffirms the Spanish gift for the audacious gesture.

155

Fiery light of round window illumines interior. Above: Mary in glory.

Massive, palisaded church sits amid bright Majorcan colors.

Ornately carved and decorated Mirador
portal of south wall with church father below.

Not far from Bhubanes-
war, in the city of Puri on
the east coast of India,
stands the famous Jagan-
nath temple dedicated to

Jagannath Temple

the Hindu god Vishnu, "beloved protector of the world." Vishnu had ten chief
avatars, or incarnations, in which he descended to earth. Jagannath, which means
"lord of the world" in Sanskrit, is one such incarnation.

Jagannath is a group of four buildings laid out on an east-to-west axis. With
its curvilinear tower, porch, and two halls, the complex lies within a double-walled
enclosure on the site of an ancient Buddhist sanctuary called Dantpura. Within the
temple sanctuary are the cult images of Jagannath, his brother Balabhadra, and his
sister Subhadra.

In June, one of the most venerated religious festivals takes place at Puri: the
Rath Yatra, or running of the car of Jagannath. Thousands of devoted believers
congregate to pay homage to Vishnu. Excitement mounts as the sixteen-wheeled
chariot starts down the main road of Puri, with the god's image riding in splendor
on a jeweled throne. Pulled by hundreds of pilgrims, the giant car picks up speed
and moves irresistibly down the mile-long route as frenzy increases. At times,
exalted devotees have thrown themselves under the wheels of the holy car, which,
at the height of the celebration, is unstoppable. (It is from the name Jagannath that
the English word "juggernaut" is derived.) At last it reaches the garden house, a
temple in which it remains for eight days until the return trip. At intervals the car
is broken up, as are the god figures, and their pieces are sold as holy relics. They
are then all fashioned anew.

159

Rath Yatra, or running of the "juggernaut." Above: Curved tower of temple complex.

Every August 5, in the great basilica popularly known as Our Lady of the Snow, a shower of white rose petals falls from the

Santa Maria Maggiore

dome within the Borghese chapel to commemorate the founding of Santa Maria Maggiore in 358. According to legend, the church owes its origin to a childless Roman patrician who decided to leave his estate to the Virgin. In a dream on the night of August 4, he was commanded to build a church on the spot where he would find snow on the Esquiline Hill. Pope Liberius that night had had a similar dream and was instructed to cooperate in the search for a site. The next day—at the height of a Roman summer—snow was found. The pope traced the outlines of a church on the ground and building immediately began.

Although it has been considerably altered over the centuries, Santa Maria preserves the character of a fourth-century basilica better than any of Rome's early churches. The most important surviving fifth-century mosaics are found in the nave and on the chancel arch. Old Testament figures relate the lives of Abraham, Jacob, Isaac, Moses, and Joshua on the wide walls. On the chancel arch, New Testament subjects include the Annunciation, Presentation in the Temple, the Adoration of the Magi, and the Massacre of the Innocents.

Within the old basilica a number of singular events took place: the body of church father St. Jerome was brought here from Bethlehem and lies buried in an unknown spot. On Christmas eve in 1538, St. Ignatius Loyola, founder of the Jesuit order, celebrated his first mass. None, however, is as evocative as the shower of white rose petals each August 5, when Santa Maria Maggiore celebrates her legend. 161

Campanile is Rome's tallest. Above: Curved steps outside apse.

Left: Statue of Pope Pius IX kneels before reliquary.

Ionic columns of nave.

High altar with crypt below.

Nave with 16th-century coffered ceiling.

The Temple of Heaven in Peking was the most sacred religious site in all of Imperial China. It consists of three main structures—the Altar of Heaven, the Hall of Prayer for Good Harvests, and the Temple of the God of the Universe—lying within a 700-acre walled enclosure that is bounded by a square in the south and a circle in the north.

Temple of Heaven

The most important religious event of the year took place at dawn on the day of the winter solstice at the Altar of Heaven. Enclosed in a square courtyard, the shrine consists of three concentric circular white marble terraces. When the worshiper moved from the square (symbolizing earth in Chinese iconography) to the circle (the motif for heaven), he figuratively journeyed from earth to heaven. As an ox roasted in a furnace below, the emperor, facing north on the topmost round, prostrated himself while addressing the supreme deity. The other great religious ceremony took place in the spring, when the emperor made his annual supplication for bountiful crops, in the Hall of Prayer for Good Harvests. This magnificent round structure is built entirely of wood and rests on twenty-eight columns. The four central pillars represent the four seasons. The remaining twenty-four columns are arranged in two circles, one group symbolizing the twelve months of the year, the other the twelve hours of the Chinese day. The interior is brilliantly painted and decorated with abstract designs. A three-tiered roof surmounts the hall.

Although secularized in 1911, when the last Manchu emperor was deposed, the Temple of Heaven still evokes the days of Imperial China when harmony between earth and heaven was considered the supreme good.

165

Temple of Prayer for Good Harvests. Above: Whispering wall.

Left and below: Ceiling pattern and exterior decoration.

Temple (rear) is approached by long avenue.

167

Cathedral of Santa Maria de la Sede

After King Ferdinand III of Castile retook Seville from the Moors in 1248, the great mosque built by Yusaf II was dedicated to *Seville Cathedral*

Santa Maria de la Sede and became the cathedral of Seville. In 1401, a decision was made to replace the mosque with "a church so vast and grand that none shall be its equal, even if those who see it completed shall think we were mad."

Begun in 1402, the vast cathedral of Seville is the largest Gothic church in Europe, exceeded in area only by St. Peter's in Rome. The elaborately carved altar screen, the largest in Spain, contains forty-five biblical scenes, each one more than a yard square, with enough sculptured figures "to populate a fair-sized medieval town." The pillars in the nave soar to a height of 132 feet. Standing just northeast of the cathedral is the Giralda tower, once the mosque's minaret, to which a Renaissance bell tower was added in the sixteenth century. The weathervane, or *giraldillo,* at the top, a bronze figure of Faith, gives the tower its name.

The cathedral houses the monumental sarcophagus of Christopher Columbus, whose bones were brought here from Havana in 1899. The sarcophagus is borne on the shoulders of four giant figures representing the kingdoms of Castile, León, Aragon, and Navarre. Within the Capilla Mayor, a chapel at the east end designed in 1550, is the bronze and silver casket of Ferdinand III, which is opened four times a year so that Seville's populace may view the body of the city's deliverer. In a small crypt below are mementoes carried by Ferdinand into battle against the Moors: his pennon, sword, and an ivory crucifix said to have been fixed to his saddle pommel.

169

Decorated vaults were rebuilt in 16th century. Above: Holy Week procession.

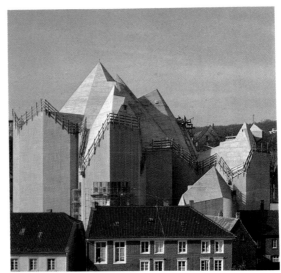

The pyramidal "tent" roofs of the huge pilgrimage church in Neviges, Germany, rise over this small town in the wooded hills of the northern Rhine-Westphalia region. Designed in 1964 by Gottfried Böhm, the church lies a short distance from the little parish church that made Neviges a renowned pilgrimage site in the seventeenth century. According to legend, Antonius Schirley, a Franciscan friar of the nearby monastery of Dorsten, was praying to a small portrait of the Virgin Mary in September, 1680, when he heard a voice speak from the picture, saying "Bring me to Hardenberg [a section of Neviges]. There I wish to be worshiped." Word soon spread about the wondrous picture and pilgrims began flocking to behold the holy portrait, which was later enshrined at the church of Neviges. The numbers of devout visitors increased over the years, and the Franciscan friars decided recently to build a new and more substantial structure. Thus in the old town, with its picturesque squares and narrow lanes, arose one of the most startling and innovative churches of the 1960's, a forty-seven-sided building that might be taken for a piece of cubist sculpture. Built of reinforced concrete, Neviges has the largest interior space, after Cologne cathedral, in the Rhineland. Immense concrete supports and balconies, in odd cubic shapes encircling the nave, give it a theatrical feeling, heightened by the dramatic placement of the pulpit, jutting out into the nave from one of the pillars.

This strikingly original church attracts 200,000 visitors annually to the little town of Neviges. The Virgin's holy portrait, which spoke to the Franciscan friar three hundred years ago, stands highlighted in the Chapel of Grace.

Pilgrimage Church of Neviges

171

Worshipers gather in vast interior. Above: Multifaceted concrete church is startling sight.

Cathedral Church of St. Mary

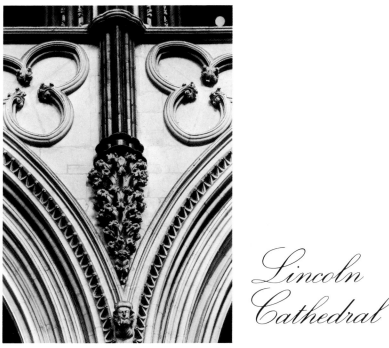

Before Rome's legions fortified the hill town of Lindum Colonia, Lincoln was a strategic Celtic settlement with a commanding

Lincoln Cathedral

view across thirty miles of flat fenland. The Roman gate at Newport Arch and the imperial roads running arrow-straight for sixteen miles along Foss Way and Ermine Street testify to Lincoln's "continuous being since ancient times." Above the summit of the hill, Lincoln's towers rise as they did centuries ago, a beacon for pilgrims who were making their way to the shrine of St. Hugh.

In 1185, an earthquake shook the hill and "cleft" the old Norman minster, a church built after the Conquest. A new church, planned in the revolutionary style of Early English Gothic, was launched in 1186 by a visionary bishop, Hugh of Avalon. Probably all that was completed in Hugh's lifetime was the eastern limb, a sumptuous work, long since gone. Hugh, a man of extraordinary character, was much loved. At his death he expressed a modest wish to be buried within the chapel of St. John the Baptist, but in a manner "to least obstruct the passage of worshippers." So great, however, was the press of pilgrims that the canons decided to rebuild the presbytery to house their beloved saint more appropriately.

Hugh's shrine disappeared long ago. But at the eastern end of the Angel Choir stands a richly detailed fourteenth-century pedestal on which once rested the saint's head in a reliquary. Outside the church, St. Hugh's carved figure rises from a pinnacle on the clifflike west front. Behind him loom Lincoln's towers. The central one, with the famous five-and-a-half-ton Tom-of-Lincoln Bell, is 271 feet high, the tallest cathedral tower in England.

173

Early English Gothic exterior was revolutionary in its time. Above: Detail of Angel Choir arcade.

The founding of the Mormons began with the dream of a seventeen-year-old boy from Palmyra, New York, Joseph

Great Mormon Temple

Smith, to whom an angel appeared "whose name was Moroni." From that dream to this temple, over which the gilt figure of the Angel Moroni blows his trumpet, a chronicle unfolds of persecution, murder, and strength of purpose.

After Smith organized the first church in Palmyra, missionaries established Mormon communities in Ohio and Missouri, but intolerance drove them ever westward. In 1844 Smith, his brother, and two other members were murdered by an angry mob in Nauvoo, Illinois. Under their new leader, Brigham Young, the Mormons began a heroic trek in quest of a "new Zion." Thousands struggled across the Continental Divide. In July, 1848, Young, looking out over a valley near what is now Salt Lake City, Utah, is reported to have said, "This is the place."

The Salt Lake temple was inspired in large part by Young. The façade is emblazoned with emblematic devices—stones, stars, torches—all thought to represent secret practices of the Masons, a sect that intrigued both Smith and Young. Inside the temple is a series of rooms used for Mormon rituals and religious teachings. The most important is the baptism room, in which stands a great copper font resting on the backs of twelve life-size oxen with silver horns. Young said of his vision of the church, "I want to see the temple built in a manner that will endure the millennium . . . to stand as a proud monument of the faith, perseverance and industry of the saints of God in the mountains of the nineteenth century." Out of their industry, the Mormons have created a monument for an age.

175

Illuminated towers of Salt Lake Temple. Above: Angel Moroni.

Agadez mosque stands in a sun-baked oasis, a caravan crossing in the West African desert republic of Niger. The mosque,

Agadez Mosque

originally built in the sixteenth century, was later restored, almost a thousand years after the Moslems had overrun the Middle East, Europe, and North Africa in their holy war to conquer the world for Allah.

In Africa, Islam spread along established trade routes and across the Sahara into western Africa. The Aïr massif and the desert around Agadez have historically been controlled by the Berber Tuaregs, a seminomadic tribe who were once undisputed lords of the Sahara. Today a Tuareg *amenokal*, or sultan, still rules an area the size of Texas from a decaying mud-brick castle near the mosque.

African mosques differ markedly from the East to the West. The eastern mosque was originally just a cleanly swept rectangular space with a line of stones delineating the ritual area. Later the Swahili, a mixture of Arab and African cultures, built more complex structures, usually of coral and cement on a rectangular ground plan above which was raised a complex system of domes. In western Africa a similar rectangular ground plan is used, but the mosque's central element is its tapering minaret. At Agadez the minaret, eighty-eight feet high, contains an interior spiral staircase braced by tamarisk logs and leading up to a balcony where the muezzin, or crier, issues the call to prayer. The mosque itself is an extremely low-roofed rectangular building with barely enough room in which to stand upright. The structure is built entirely of mud brick. Its outer boundaries are marked by a low-walled courtyard beyond which stretches the vastness of the Sahara.

177

Faithful (above) are called to prayer from Agadez's mud-brick minaret.

Twice each summer Siena puts on medieval costume and runs the *palio,* a horse race with its roots in the Middle Ages. Ri-

Siena Cathedral

ders carrying the colors and emblems of various city districts slash at each other with whips as they clatter round the cathedral's cobbled piazza. During the week of the *palio,* the victor's banner is brought ceremoniously to the cathedral. Preceded by drums and bells, the cart, drawn by four white oxen, enters the piazza of the *duomo,* while the archbishop, his priests, and the church choir await the procession on the steps of the cathedral's west front.

Siena's façade, begun around 1284 by Giovanni Pisano, stands in the front rank of Italian Gothic achievements. The new style developed its essential Italian character in Tuscany. Multicolored marble clothes the exterior. The black and white marble banding lends the cathedral its exotic zebra-stripe look. The interior is an expanse of marble marked by spaciousness and light. The floor engaged more than forty artists from 1372 to 1562. No less celebrated is Pisano's pulpit, probably one of the greatest works of medieval sculpture in Italy.

Around 1339 Siena started to rebuild the cathedral, intending to double its size, but the Black Death intervened. Eighty thousand people, a third of the populace, died. The city never recovered. Today the *palio* procession is a reminder of Siena's great past, such as the day in 1311 when the city turned out to lead the new altarpiece by Duccio di Buoninsegna to the cathedral. The archival record of the event ends with this note: "Lire 12, soldi 10, paid to the sound of trumpets, cymbals, and drums for having gone to meet the said picture."

179

Glowing marble façade was begun in 13th century. Above: "Zebra-striped" campanile.

Richly appointed altar.

Church of San Carlo Borromeo

The Holy Roman emperor Charles VI had vowed that if Vienna were delivered from the plague, he would build a great *Karlskirche*

church. Karlskirche, commissioned in 1716 and named for the ecclesiastical reformer San Carlo Borromeo, honors that vow. Sited originally on a grassy knoll overlooking the city, it is now surrounded by urban sprawl but remains an imposing example of early Austrian Baroque.

Its architect, Johann Bernhard Fischer von Erlach, was trained in Rome and brought back with him traditional classical elements that were incorporated in his façade at Karlskirche. Fischer von Erlach established his reputation at Salzburg with the first of his so-called Roman Baroque churches, but Karlskirche is his ecclesiastical masterpiece. The touch of genius is in the two colossal columns flanking the portico. The spiral design is derived from Trajan's column in Rome. It is said also to suggest columns that reportedly stood outside Solomon's temple in Jerusalem. The deliverance of Vienna by the intercession of San Carlo provides the main decorative theme, scenes from the saint's life curving up each column.

Initially the architect's plan suggested a more austere interior, but when his son Joseph Emanuel took over after Fischer von Erlach's death, certain heightened theatrical effects were introduced. The blending of fresco painting with stucco figures, a quintessentially Baroque feature in which at times one cannot tell where the sculpture ends and the painting begins, is best illustrated in the high altar ensemble. Karlskirche, Fisher von Erlach's attempt to create a style of Imperial Baroque, represents the unique vision of one man.

183

Unique columns flank portico. Above: Flamboyant oval dome.

St. Andrew's Church

Built around 1250 in the Sogne Fjord area of Norway, Borgund's "stave church" is the best preserved of these medieval *Stave Church of Borgund* masterpieces. These all-wooden buildings get their name from the massive upright timbers that are a basic part of their construction. About thirty stave churches survive out of some thousand believed to have existed in the Middle Ages. Shingled and ornamented with dragon-head carvings, the churches were popularly called "scale-covered monsters" in the nineteenth century.

The *drakkar* on the topmost roof of Borgund's church also appeared on the prows of Viking ships in the ninth and tenth centuries. With the introduction of Christianity into Norway about 1000, there was a gradual blending of pagan and Christian designs. Figured carvings and paintings began to appear for the first time. Floral motifs were borrowed from holy books brought over by English missionaries. Borgund's portal is remarkable for its elaborate carvings of intertwined snakes in a floral design, as well as for the decorative use of ninth-century runic characters, taken from an ancient Norse language written in spikey script.

The Norwegian stave churches were largely unknown to the outside world until their discovery in the early nineteenth century by J. C. Dahl, a painter and teacher. Little is known of their origins, though some scholars suggest that they are adaptations of the primitive *hov,* or hall, written about in the Viking sagas. Others claim that they are adaptations in wood of the single-naved Anglo-Saxon *kirkehus,* or church-house. Most agree, however, that the ancient Norse gods Thor and Odin were worshiped in such stave buildings before the coming of Christianity.

A medieval masterpiece in wood. Above: Drakkar *roof ornament.*

Cathedral of St. Peter

Cologne Cathedral

Cologne took longer to build than any other medieval cathedral. Archbishop Conrad van Hochstaden, eager to provide an appropriate setting for the city's esteemed collection of relics, began the work by pulling down the old Carolingian basilica. The east end of the new cathedral went up relatively quickly, between 1248 and 1322. The chancel, the first part completed, is remarkably preserved, especially its frescoes and choir stalls, which are as vibrant in color today as they were when Petrarch wrote of them after a visit in 1333.

Thereafter, work went on sporadically. The west front was begun in the mid-fourteenth century, the south tower went up to the belfry by 1473. But lack of funds, political disputes, and the disruptions of the Hundred Years' War impeded progress, and by 1560 construction had come to a halt. A crane standing atop the unfinished south tower was a landmark for nearly three hundred years. Nave pillars rose only to the level of the capitals, stumps remained in the ground for the north tower. Even the French Revolution added insult when the cathedral was sacked and reduced to a hay store by the invading "People's Army."

Not until the Gothic Revival movement in the nineteenth century was interest in the gigantic torso reawakened. The original drawing for the west front was found stretched over a frame for drying beans. In 1880, more than six hundred years after it was begun, completion of the great cathedral was celebrated.

Cologne is the largest Gothic cathedral in northern Europe, only Milan and Seville being larger. Seen from any point in the city, or as disembodied spires rising out of the early-morning mist, it is unforgettable.

187

Cathedral took six centuries to complete. Above: Figures in façade.

Triptych: Masterwork by Lochner.

Elaborately carved choir stalls.

Left: Piers of double-aisled nave, from triforium.

189

In the sixth century B.C., a reaction against Hinduism, brought about largely because of exploitation by the priestly class, led to the reform movement of Jainism, with its particular emphasis on *ahimsa,* or nonviolence, and asceticism. The Jains' fundamental creed is absolute reverence for life. They will not even till the soil for fear of injuring insects.

Mount Abu

Early in their history, the Jains began placing shrines on mountaintops. Many of these lofty sites became temple cities known as "mountains of immortality." One of the most spectacular complexes is Mount Abu, which rises 4,000 feet near the village of Dilwara, in Rajasthan, India. Two of the finest examples of surviving Jain temples are found in this complex—the Vimala, built in 1031 and named for its founder, the governor of the state; and the Tejpal, ascribed to a Jain who erected it in 1230 in memory of his brother Vastupala. According to an ancient inscription, the Tejpal is said to be unrivaled in India for its "delicacy of carving and beauty of detail, even in a land known for patience and lavish labor."

The white marble temple lies within a rectangular, high-walled enclosure composed of cells, each of which holds the seated figure of a *jina,* or Jain saint. The temple itself is dedicated to Neminath, the twenty-second *jina,* whose image is housed in the dimly lit sanctuary. Behind the shrine are sculptured figures of the family of Vahamana, the sect's founder. Nearby are five elaborately carved elephants with harnesses and trappings of incredible delicacy. The sumptuous effect of Jain carvings is seen best on the central cupola, where sixteen four-armed goddesses encircle the dome, which is said to rival the work of the finest Gothic sculptors.

191

Temple is profusely decorated with intricate carving. Above: Detail of goddess.

Cathedral of St. James

Built between 1078 and 1211 and the unarguable masterpiece of Spanish Romanesque, Santiago de Compostela, or St. *Santiago de Compostela*

James's cathedral, was the quintessential pilgrimage church of the eleventh century. Its immense nave accommodated the continuous flow of pilgrims rounding the ambulatory near the saint's shrine at the east end. Chapels were added as way stations for those making the circuit. The silver casket in a ninth-century crypt below the high altar contains the saint's remains. According to tradition, a band of Spanish disciples brought the apostle's body back from Palestine after his beheading in 46 A.D. and buried him at a spot near Santiago. The site was somehow lost and forgotten until stars hovering over the sacred place led to its rediscovery in 813. Thereafter it was known as the Field of the Stars, or *Campus Stellae.*

The first church there, a humble affair, was razed by the Moslem vizier al-Mansur, who led a coastal attack in 997 that destroyed the little town of Santiago. Over these ancient ruins arose the present cathedral, whose Baroque western front, added in the seventeenth and eighteenth centuries, little prepares one for the austerity within. The Spartan interior seems to move one forward toward the rich shrine and the bejeweled thirteenth-century figure of the saint, whose mantle has been worn down by the kisses of the devout. Saint James's scallop-shell emblem is seen over the main doors of the church. Found everywhere en route to Santiago, figures of the emblem are bought by tourists as souvenirs. Once, on pain of excommunication, they could be made and sold only within the city, so that none but a true pilgrim might proudly display his badge of devotion on returning home.

Left: Saint's emblem over portals. Above: Saint's day fete.

Sumptuously gilded altar contrasts . . .

Holy Week celebration.

. . . with relatively severe nave.

Bejeweled effigy of St. James.

Swinging the giant censer.

195

On Japan's largest island, Honshu, in a grove of camphor trees just outside the town of Yamada, stands Ise Naiku, the ho-

Ise Shrine

liest shrine of the Shinto religion. A complex of four buildings in a large rectangular compound, it is enclosed by four fences, one inside the other. The shrine, which was founded late in the third century, is dedicated to Amaterasu, the sun goddess. Built of yellow cypress, the thatched-roofed structures are raised on piles seven feet off the ground. The main building, where only the emperor and high priest may enter, lies behind the innermost fence. In this *Shoden* are housed the three sacred treasures of the Japanese throne: the mirror, symbol of Amaterasu; the jewel; and the sword. The priests' meeting hall lies between the first and second fences.

The practice of Shintoism, an ancient religion that combines nature worship with ancestor worship, is the simplest communion of men and gods. At the shrine priests service this communion through unpretentious morning and evening rituals consisting of offerings of food to the deity, followed by recitations. When worshipers arrive, they wash their hands at small shrines and pavilions before entering the first enclosure. Approaching the second gate, they clap sharply to announce their presence. Then, permitted no further, they withdraw for prayer and meditation.

In keeping with a tradition begun during the reign of Emperor Temmu (673–86), the entire complex is torn down and reconstructed every twenty years. This periodic renewal has so depleted the imperial forest in the Kiso Mountains of yellow cypress trees that future rebuildings may have to rely heavily on Korean and Taiwanese timber.

197

Worn steps lead to 3rd-century shrine. Above: Meditation.

Four fences, pierced by portals, enclose shrine.
Worshipers are forbidden beyond second.

198

Sacred buildings (above) are attended by Shinto priests (below).

Durham cathedral, England's great Anglo-Norman church, is superbly sited on a bluff overlooking the River Wear.

Durham Cathedral

Viewed from the southwest, a view considered one of the most spectacular in Britain, the forward part of the cathedral is the Galilee Chapel, a large porch that has been turned into a Lady Chapel. As a rule, the Lady Chapel is placed at the east end of a cathedral. Legend has it, however, that Durham's resident saint, Cuthbert (d. 687), so detested women that every time the chapel was begun near his tomb at the eastern end he caused the foundation to collapse.

Presenting its north face to Scotland, a border often overrun by Scottish raiders, Durham was said to be "half church of God, half castle 'gainst the Scot," one of a series of strongholds built by William the Conquerer. Begun in 1093 and largely completed by 1220, it was the first church to use ribbed stone vaulting throughout. Within, the immense columns alternating with unadorned piers lend the interior a monumentality offset by the deeply incised patterns on each rounded pier: vertical and spiral fluting, chevrons, and a diamond or square design called a diaper. The chevron, a motif seen throughout Norman England, decorates virtually every surface in Durham—ribs, arches, moldings. Though the pointed arches and ribbed vaults are a harbinger of Gothic, the church is wholly Romanesque.

From as early as 995, when the church was made of "wands and branches," the pilgrims' goal had been St. Cuthbert's shrine. In 1104 the shrine was moved behind the high altar. Even here monks spared the misogynous saint the presence of women, who were not allowed beyond a black marble line still visible today.

201

"Half castle 'gainst the Scot." Above: Sanctuary door knocker.

Towers at west front.

Chevron arches of Galilee chapel.

Left: Durham was first to use rib vaulting throughout.

Bhubaneswar, in the state of Orissa in eastern India, is a city of temples. Some say there were once seven hundred of them. Accord-

Lingaraja Temple

ing to legend, Bhubaneswar was on the site of a great forest of mango trees sacred to the followers of Vishnu, who with Brahma and Shiva is one of the main gods of the Hindu pantheon. Shiva, Lord of the Cosmic Dance, restorer and destroyer of life, was worshiped in the city of Benares, but became unhappy with its sinful ways and sought to move into Vishnu's grove. Vishnu agreed on condition that Shiva cut all ties with Benares. Reluctant at first to give up the myriad sanctuaries and temples of the holy city, Shiva was persuaded when Vishnu assured him that he would find all these needs in the holy forest. Shiva moved into Bhubaneswar, where, as procreator, he was worshiped in the form of a lingam, or stylized phallus.

Bhubaneswar is a complex of some five hundred temples of which Lingaraja is the largest. It consists of four buildings laid out on a straight east-west axis. Two of these are the earliest temple structures, dating from about 1000. The Sri Mandir (or towered sanctuary) houses the god's cult object, the lingam.

On a small island in the adjoining sacred pool, the Bindu Sarouar, there is a sanctuary where once a year the image of the god is immersed in the holy water. At the annual festival of Shivarati, Shiva's night, held in late February, the temples gleam in torchlight, the lingam is anointed with ghee (clarified butter) and garlanded with flowers. Later a priest carrying torches runs through the crowds of pilgrims and climbs to the tower's top, signaling the end of fasting and beginning of feasting. Lingaraja serves only high-caste Hindus. Outsiders are not permitted in the temple.

205

Lingaraja, largest of Bhubaneswar's 500 temples. Above: Heavenly maiden.

Probably the greatest architectural heritage of the late Middle Ages in England lies not in any single great structure, but in the

St. Mary's Parish Church

countless parish churches built primarily in the Gothic Perpendicular style. Until the late fourteenth century most parish churches were relatively small and insignificant. But as small freeholders prospered, especially where the wool trade flourished in the Cotswolds, the emerging merchant class gave impetus to building larger and more highly ornamented parish churches. St. Mary's in Fairford, in the lovely unspoiled Gloucestershire Cotswolds, is a typical "wool church."

With the decline of monasticism after the Reformation, rural life centered increasingly around the parish church. Local benefactors began to establish chantries, or small chapels, as family memorials. In the sixteenth century John Tame, a prosperous wool merchant, left the church at Fairford a large sum of money in his will for reconstruction on a grand scale. The tombs of John Tame, his wife Alice, and his son, Sir Edmund Tame, lie within, covered by exceptional brass effigies.

The central feature of the church is its twenty-eight stained-glass windows, believed to have come from the same Anglo-Flemish workshop that produced the extraordinary glass of Kings College Chapel at Cambridge. They are the only intact cluster of such windows known to have survived the Puritan raids of Oliver Cromwell's time. They depict a biblical narrative cycle from the Creation to the Last Judgment, which is known for its blast-furnace "hell mouth," multicolored devils, and grotesque Satan. St. Mary's is also an outstanding example of Gloucestershire masonry—the finest stone craftsmen developed their skill in this area.

207

Graveyard and Gothic Perpendicular facade. Above: Detail of Last Judgment window.

In the town of Aylesford, in the heart of Nova Scotia's Annapolis Valley, St. Mary's of Auburn stands like a white steepled out- *St. Mary's Church*

post against the flat countryside. Situated now on a crossroads leading to the principal cities of Halifax and Annapolis Royal, it reflects the character of a pioneer Georgian church built when Aylesford was still a forested frontier town.

The French Acadians who settled Nova Scotia established one of their major encampments at Port Royal. After their land was ceded to the British in 1713, it was resettled by Anglicans and Dissenters. These early English settlers, under the leadership of Charles Inglis, first bishop of Nova Scotia, erected St. Mary's church to serve both as a religious center and a political and cultural meeting place.

St. Mary's was designed by Bishop Inglis and master builder William Matthews. A shortage of lime for the masonry and plaster work gave rise to one of the most intriguing stories connected with the church. In 1755–56 fugitive Acadians wintering at French Cross on the Bay of Fundy, seven miles away, kept themselves alive by eating mussels. Thirty-five years later the mussel shells they left were pounded into powdered lime and used in the plaster of the church walls. St. Mary's is sometimes referred to as the "mussel-shell church." Typically Georgian are the single round-head windows and the simple classical ornamentation around door and tower. All, however, is reduced in scale to suit the needs of a frontier town.

In the old graveyard, James Morden, the founder of St. Mary's, lies in the northeast corner. Around him are the remains of the pioneers who helped raise the church the bishop said would "grace any village in England."

Classical hall church interior. Above: Delicate steeple dominates façade.

Near the natural springs that gave the city of Wells its name is one of England's smallest but loveliest cathedrals. The spring

Wells Cathedral

still bubbles up in the bishop's garden where St. Andrew's dominates the Somerset countryside. To the west, it presents one of the most remarkable façades in England.

A supreme example of the doctrinal screen, the west façade is some 147 feet wide, a great cliff of carved figures stretching beyond the aisles and around the sides of the towers. Of the four hundred original figures, more than half are gone, most destroyed in the puritanical fervor of the Reformation. Among the sculpture that remains are some of the best medieval figures in England.

Begun around 1186, Wells is only sixty-seven feet high, modest in comparison with the immense vaults of the French. What it lacks in size is more than made up by the poetic detail of its interior. England's native gift for small carving is splendidly displayed on capitals and on corbels in the transepts. Vignettes of medieval life, scenes from nature, animal heads, and crisply undercut stylized leaves appear everywhere.

Perhaps the most dramatic sight at Wells is that of the nave's massive "strainer arches," an inverted archway under the tower crossing that has supported the tower for more than six hundred years. In 1338 the builders overreached themselves, and the mason discovered that the center tower had grown too heavy for its supports. To prevent a collapse, huge scissor arches were introduced on the west, north, and south sides of the tower. They have been called the "most bizarre and sensational structure in all Gothic architecture."

211

Façade's surviving figures are among England's best. Above: Window detail.

Left: For six centuries, unusual "strainer arches" have supported tower.

Column's leafy border is typical Wells detail.

Closeup of inverted arch.

The steeple of St. Michael's Episcopal church has dominated the Charleston, South Carolina, skyline since it went up in 1752–53. A contemporary noted that because of its 186-foot height, it was a boon to navigators, "who see it long before they make out any part of the land." In the War of Independence, the Colonial rebels tried to disguise it by painting it black, but the British claimed it became even more visible and lobbed shells at it.

$\mathscr{St.\,Michael's}$
$\mathscr{Church}$

St. Michael's is the second church on the site, and the oldest in Charleston. As the Establishment church, St. Michael's served both secular and religious needs. A prerevolutionary polling place during elections, it was also the forum for public discussion of such civic matters as fortifying the coast, whether to build a new frigate, and defense during the War of 1812. During the Civil War, Union shells once struck the west front as the congregation was leaving. The famed "ring" of eight bells, which had been sent to Columbia for safekeeping, ironically were reduced to molten lumps when Sherman set a torch to that city. Later recast, the bells were hung once again in the old church.

Typical of Georgian churches in the South, St. Michael's is built of white stucco brick, fronted by a two-story portico with four Doric columns. Surmounted by a massive tower, it is topped by a seven-and-a-half-foot weathervane. In the rectangular nave are many of the original furnishings: the beautifully carved pulpit, the chandelier that held forty-two candles when first brought from London in 1803, and the box pews, one of which was used by George Washington during a state visit in 1791.

215

Steeple has been beacon to navigators. Above: Triumphant saint.

Nine miles south of Tucson, Arizona, on a low rise over the Santa Cruz Valley, stands San Xavier del Bac. Stark white against *San Xavier del Bac*

the dusty mesquite, it is like a gleaming mirage in its desert setting. The Indians call it *La Paloma Blanca del Desierto*—"The White Dove of the Desert."

Begun in 1784 by a group of Franciscan friars led by Juan Bautista Velderrain, San Xavier is considered the most ambitious of all Spanish Colonial churches. The padres, working with brick and mortar, could not have built so elegant a structure without trained labor. Skilled craftsmen, especially for the finer work, had to be imported—in all likelihood from Mexico, though no one knows for certain. Little is known of the actual construction, and even the architect's identity is a mystery. However, on the door of the sacristy a name and date are roughly burned in: "Pedro Boj, 1797." Perhaps Boj was the master mason at San Xavier.

The church is built on a Latin cross plan, with nave, transepts, and apse at the east end, covered by five low brick domes not visible from the outside. The interior is lavishly decorated with carved stone, woodwork, molded plaster, and murals. Dominating the façade is an ornately sculptured central panel of red brick. Although the west tower has a small dome and lantern, the east is unfinished. The story goes that one of the friars fell to his death as he prepared to lay stones for the dome, and that the tower was left unfinished as his monument.

On the volutes, the curved scrolls at each side of the front, San Xavier's builder carved a cat and mouse that glare at each other across the width of the gable. The Indians say, "When cat catches mouse, the end of the world will come."

Cat and mouse crouch in façade's curved scrolls. Above: Name and date on sacristy door.

Left: Ornate interior centers on effigy of the saint.

"White Dove of the Desert."

Brick-red panel is strong contrast.

Santa Maria del Fiore

Seen from the hills around Florence, the cathedral's great dome soars, and a finger of the Palazzo Vecchio tower stabs the sky.

Florence Cathedral

Both share the skyline as they did at the time of the Renaissance. In 1224, surrounded by rival cities, each outbuilding the other with grander churches, the Florentine commune determined to build a new cathedral that would be "more beautiful than any other in the region of Tuscany." Arnolfo di Cambio, Italy's greatest medieval builder, was commissioned to build the church.

Arnolfo's plan, only partly realized in his lifetime, was a design of "colossal simplicity" with four great arches supporting the nave, and a huge central space. Giotto, who succeeded Arnolfo as master of the works, added his celebrated campanile, or bell tower. Dominating the pink, green, and white Gothic façade of Santa Maria del Fiore, Brunelleschi's incomparable dome was acknowledged as the finest European architectural achievement since Rome's Pantheon. The dome was at first thought too huge to be supported. But Brunelleschi's double-shell construction, the first such use of masonry, provided a brilliant solution to an age-old engineering problem. A century later, when Michelangelo left Florence for Rome to work on St. Peter's, he stopped for a last look at Brunelleschi's masterpiece and said, "I can do nothing more beautiful." Gothic in form, Renaissance in spirit, the cathedral, dome, campanile, and baptistery form one of the unique complexes in the history of church architecture. The poet Dante was baptized in the baptistery, and the east doors, masterpieces of gilded bas-reliefs by Lorenzo Ghiberti, were called the "Gates of Paradise" by Michelangelo.

221

Monumental dome by Brunelleschi. Above: Self-portrait of Ghiberti carved in "Gates of Paradise."

Left: Angled view of façade, with bell tower in foreground.

Ceiling mosaics in baptistery dome.

Left front portal.

One of the best-known and best-loved landmarks in New York City is St. Patrick's cathedral. It may even be the most fa-

St. Patrick's Cathedral

mous Catholic church in the country. When construction was begun in 1858 on Fifth Avenue, between 50th and 51st Streets, the site held only one major building, a Trappist monks' orphanage. The cost of the lot, "with improvements," was $11,000. Today the block on which the church stands is valued at $14,000,000.

James Renwick, who was commissioned to build St. Patrick's, was expected to put up the largest church ever erected in the United States. The cathedral is stylistically a Gothic composite. The west façade, with twin towers, rose window, and triple portals, reflects its French medieval heritage. Within, Renwick's "forest of marble columns" comes mainly from English Decorated Gothic. The groin roof, with its decorative ribs like so many great English vaults, rises 112 feet. Visitors craning their necks are often startled to see suspended from ornamental bosses the hats of late cardinals of the church. These wide-brimmed *galeros* are given to each newly elected cardinal by the pope. On the cardinal's death, his *galero* is hung within his cathedral, over his crypt, remaining there until it disintegrates.

The emotional impact of St. Patrick's, noted a contemporary, "is in the cavernous interior always gently astir with the flickering banks of candles, the murmur of masses, and the coming and going of tourists and the devout. In addition to its day-to-day service it provides a matchless setting for great religious ceremonies. . . . Since its opening St. Patrick's has served in the fullest sense as a great urban cathedral."

225

Aerial view shows Latin cross plan. Above: Center portal on west façade.

Left: Easter service.

Sermon from the pulpit.

"Flickering banks of candles."

Terence Cardinal Cooke celebrates mass.

Worshiper receives communion.

In seventeenth-century Japan, corrupt Buddhist priests attached to the Honganji temple in Kyoto incurred the displeasure

Higashi Honganji Temple

of the reigning shogun, or ruler, Ieyasu of Tokugowa. Ieyasu set out to divest the priests of their power by splitting the sect in two. In 1692 he erected a new temple, the Higashi Honganji, or eastern temple, some distance from the earlier Nishi, or western temple. These are now the holiest sites of Japan's largest Buddhist sect, the Jodo-Shinsu.

When the call went out for contributions to help build the Higashi Honganji, many responded. Those without money gave lumber and stone, time and labor. But the fervor of Japanese women led to an act of devotion that remains unparalleled. Untold thousands cut off their long black hair, out of which were woven twenty-nine enormous *kezuna,* or human-hair ropes, used to hoist the pillars and roof beams into place. The largest of these cables is said to have been two hundred feet long and about sixteen inches around.

Higashi Honganji consists of two main structures linked by a covered corridor, the Great Hall (Daishi-do) and a subsidiary building (the Amido-do). The Great Hall, one of the largest temples in Japan, has an immense, upturned, double-tiered roof that can be seen from any point in Kyoto. The gilded interior, where a figure of Kenshin Daisa, founder of the sect, is enshrined, is dimly lit by light entering through the *shoji,* or paper panels. Above the altar are angels of the Buddhist heaven, phoenixes, and other mythological figures. The floor is covered with 550 cushions on which several thousand worshipers a day are said to sit.

229

Fountain plays before Great Hall. Above: Woman at prayer.

Left: Temple attracts thousands of worshipers each day.

Double-tiered roof is focal point in Kyoto.

View of subsidiary structures.

231

According to Marcel Breuer, who designed St. Francis de Sales in 1961 with his associate Herbert Beckhardt, the great banner front of the church in Muskegon, Michigan, tells simply what it is, "like the banners by which medieval crusaders were identified." St. Francis was designed to reflect ideas growing out of the liturgical revival, a half-century of debate over the intelligibility of the Latin liturgy in modern times. "Straightforwardness" and "the honest use of material" were among the most important precepts in the search for a structure that would reflect the simplified liturgy.

Architecturally, St. Francis de Sales represents a new style of the 1950's, sometimes referred to as Brutalism, in which weight, massiveness, and the use of exposed materials are the principal features. The church is built of frankly exposed, unadorned, architectural concrete, 7,000 cubic yards of it reinforced by 575 tons of steel. The only concession to ornament is in the patterning left by form boards that held the poured concrete: rectangular shapes on the front, multiple-ridged striations at the sides. The massive altar table stands alone in the center of the sanctuary. Above it hangs the canopy, an immense slab of concrete, suspended, it seems, almost miraculously. An unusual feature of the sanctuary is the Chapel for the Blessed Sacrament, approached by a flight of steps, which is raised and inset in the rear of the sanctuary wall in full view of all worshipers. Discreet theatrical lighting can highlight either chapel or altar.

For Breuer, the story of this church is simple: "There the structure stands, its story told by the eternal laws of geometry, gravity, space."

St. Francis de Sales

233

Altar, canopy, and sanctuary. Above: Stations of Cross in atrium wall.

Exterior: Wooden forms gave pattern and texture to poured-concrete surface.

Bibliography

Adair, John, *The Pilgrim's Way*. London: Thames & Hudson, 1978.

Briggs, Morton Shaw, *Baroque Architecture*. New York: McBride, Nast, 1914.

Brown, Percy, *Indian Architecture*. Bombay: Taraporevala Sons, 1965.

Bruggink, Donald J., and Droppers, Carl H., *Christ and Architect*. Grand Rapids, Mich.: William B. Eerdmans, 1965.

Bruggink, Donald J., and Droppers, Carl H., *When Faith Takes Form*. Grand Rapids, Mich.: William B. Eerdmans, 1971.

Christ-Janer, Albert, and Foley, Mary Mix, *Modern Church Architecture*. New York: McGraw-Hill, 1962.

Collins, George R., *Antonio Gaudí*. New York: George Braziller, 1960.

Conant, Kenneth John, *Carolingian and Romanesque Architecture: 800–1200*, 2nd ed. Baltimore: Penguin Books, 1974.

Conant, Kenneth John, *The Early Architectural History of the Cathedral of Santiago de Compostela*. Cambridge, Mass.: Harvard University Press, 1926.

De Breffny, Brian, *The Synagogue*. New York: Macmillan, 1978.

Denyer, Susan, *African Traditional Architecture*. New York: Holmes & Meier, 1978.

Deva, Krishna, *Temples of North India*. New Delhi: National Book Trust, 1969.

Ditchfield, P. H., *The Cathedrals of Great Britain*. London: J. M. Dent, 1904.

Drexler, Arthur, *The Architecture of Japan*. New York: Museum of Modern Art, 1955.

Fairbank, John K., Reischauer, Edwin O., and Craig, Albert M., *East Asia: Tradition and Transformation*. Boston: Houghton Mifflin, 1973.

Federal Writers Project of the Works Progress Administration for the State of Vermont, *Vermont: A Guide to the Green Mountain State*. Boston: Houghton Mifflin, 1937.

Fitchen, John, *The Construction of Gothic Cathedrals*. Oxford: Clarendon Press, 1961.

Focillon, Henri, *The Art of the West in The Middle Ages*. 2 vols. New York: Phaidon Press, 1963.

Frankl, Paul, *Gothic Architecture*, trans. by Dieter Pevsner. Baltimore: Penguin Books, 1962.

Frédéric, Louis, *The Art of India*, trans. by Eva M. Hooykaas and A. H. Christie. New York: Harry N. Abrams, 1959.

Gerster, Georg, *Churches in Rock*. New York: Phaidon Press, 1970.

Great Religions of the World. Washington, D.C.: National Geographic Society, 1978.

Heydenreich, Ludwig H., and Lotz, Wolfgang, *Architecture in Italy: 1400–1600*. Baltimore: Penguin Books, 1974.

Hitchcock, Henry-Russel, *Architecture: Nineteenth and Twentieth Centuries*. Baltimore: Penguin Books, 1958.

Hoag, John A., *Islamic Architecture*. New York: Harry N. Abrams, 1976.

Joedicke, Jurgen, *A History of Modern Architecture*. New York: Praeger, 1959.

Kidder Smith, G. E., *The New Churches of Europe*. New York: Holt, Rinehart and Winston, 1964.

Krautheimer, Richard, *Early Christian and Byzantine Architecture*. Baltimore: Penguin Books, 1965.

Mathews, Thomas F., *The Early Churches of Constantinople: Architecture and Liturgy.* University Park: Pennsylvania State University Press, 1971.

Morrison, Hugh Sinclair, *Early American Architecture from the First Colonial Settlements to the National Period.* New York: Oxford University Press, 1952.

Morton, H. V., *In Search of England.* New York: Robert M. McBride, 1928.

Morton, H. V., *A Stranger in Spain.* New York: Dodd, Mead, 1955.

Morton, H. V., *A Traveller in Rome.* New York: Dodd, Mead, 1957.

Mullen, Robert, *The Latter-day Saints: The Mormons Yesterday and Today.* Garden City, N.Y.: Doubleday, 1966.

Murray, Peter, *Architecture of the Renaissance.* New York: Harry N. Abrams, 1971.

Norberg-Schulz, Christian, *Meaning in Western Architecture.* New York: Praeger, 1975.

Norwich, John Julius, ed., *Great Architecture of the World.* New York: Random House/American Heritage, 1975.

Paine, Robert, and Soper, Alexander, *The Art and Architecture of Japan.* Baltimore: Penguin Books, 1960.

Pevsner, Nikolaus, *An Outline of European Architecture,* 7th ed. Baltimore: Penguin Books, 1970.

Powell, Nicolas, *From Baroque to Rococo: An Introduction to Austrian and German Architecture from 1580–1790.* London: Faber & Faber, 1959.

Rosten, Leo, ed., *Religions of America.* New York: Simon & Schuster, 1975.

Schug-Wille, Christa, *Art of the Byzantine World,* trans. by E. M. Hatt. New York: Harry N. Abrams, 1969.

Sickman, Lawrence, and Soper, Alexander, *The Art and Architecture of China,* 3rd ed. Baltimore: Penguin Books, 1968.

Smith, Earl Baldwin, *The Dome.* Princeton: Princeton University Press, 1970.

Swaan, Wim, *The Gothic Cathedral.* Garden City, N.Y.: Doubleday, 1969.

Thiry, Paul, Bennet, Richard M., and Kamphoefner, Henry L., *Churches and Temples.* New York: Reinhold, 1953.

Toker, Franklin, *The Church of Notre Dame in Montreal.* Montreal: McGill University Press, 1970.

Vasari, Giorgio, *The Lives of the Painters, Sculptors and Architects.* New York: E. P. Dutton, 1927.

Whiffen, Marcus, *American Architecture Since 1780: A Guide to Styles.* Cambridge, Mass.: M.I.T. Press, 1969.

White, John, *Art and Architecture in Italy, 1250–1400.* Baltimore: Penguin Books, 1966.

Wischnitzer, Rachel, *The Architecture of the European Synagogue.* Philadelphia: Jewish Publication Society of America, 1964.

Wischnitzer, Rachel, *Synagogue Architecture in the United States.* Philadelphia: Jewish Publication Society of America, 1955.

Wu, Nelson I., *Chinese and Indian Architecture.* New York: George Braziller, 1963.

Yarwood, Doreen, *The Architecture of Europe.* New York: Hastings House, 1974.

Zarnecki, George, *Art of the Medieval World.* New York: Harry N. Abrams, 1975.

Picture Credits

12–13, 14–15: Wim Swaan. 16: Raghubir Singh. 17: Robert Lee II. 18: Rod Hanna/Woodfin Camp. 19: (top) Michael Kirtley; (btm) Rod Hanna/Woodfin Camp. 20–21: Joseph C. Farber. 22–23: Consulate General of the Netherlands. 24: C M Dixon. 25: Wim Swaan. 26: (top & btm rt) Wim Swaan; (btm left) Thomas Nebbia. 27: Thomas Nebbia. 28: David Rubinger. 29: Hubert Kanus/BV. 30: Marvin Newman/Woodfin Camp. 31: (top) Marvin Newman/Woodfin Camp; (btm) Rainer Fieselmann/BV. 32: Robert J. Forsyth. 33: F. Harlan Hambright/Design Photography. 34–35: Michael Vaccaro/Louis Mercier. 36–37: Ram Panjabi. 38: John de Visser. 39: (top & btm left) Ann & Bury Peerless; (btm rt) Ram Panjabi. 40–41: Paul Elek Ltd. 42–43: Ted Spiegel/Black Star. 44–45: Michael Kuh. 46–47: David Rubinger. 48: John de Visser. 49: Robert Estall. 50–51: (left) C M Dixon; (rt) Robert Estall. 52–53: Albert Squillace. 54: Hed Wiesner/BV. 55: Klaus M. Lang/BV. 56–57: Raymond Cauchetier. 58: Jean Dieuzaide. 59: Wim Swaan. 60–61: (top left) Paul Elek Ltd; (btm left) Jean Dieuzaide; (rt) Wim Swaan. 62: George Mott. 63: John de Visser. 64: Wim Swaan/Camera Press. 65: Fred Maroon/Louis Mercier. 66–67: (left) Michael Vaccaro/Louis Mercier; (top rt) Wim Swaan; (btm rt) Ronald Sheridan. 68–69: Thomas Haar. 70: (top) Thomas Haar; (btm) Gordon Gahan. 71: Gordon Gahan. 72–73, 74–75: Victor Englebert. 76–77, 78–79: John de Visser. 80: Victor Englebert. 81: Eduardo Comesaña. 82–83: Warren Scott. 84: British Tourist Authority. 85: James Austin. 86–87: Albie Walton. 88: Bob Davis. 89: Paul Elek Ltd. 90–91: Bob Davis. 92: John Launois/Black Star. 93: Wim Swaan. 94: John Launois/Black Star. 95: (top left) John Launois/Black Star; (top rt) Fred Maroon/Louis Mercier; (btm) Joachim Messerschmidt/BV. 96: Albert Squillace. 97: Emil Muench. 98: (top left) C M Dixon; (top rt & btm) Albert Squillace. 99: Fritz Lang/BV. 100: K. Kummels/BV. 101: Helen Marcus. 102–103: (top left & btm left) Carl Purcell; (rt) Fred Maroon/Louis Mercier. 104: George Mott. 105: Yivo Institute for Jewish Research. 106: John de Visser. 107: Karl Kernberger. 108: Adam Woolfitt/Woodfin Camp. 109: G E Kidder Smith. 110: Schmid-Tannwald/BV. 111: (top) Adam Woolfitt/Woodfin Camp; (btm left) Wim Swaan/Camera Press; (btm rt) Leonore Ander/BV. 112–113: Joseph C. Farber. 114: Adam Woolfitt/Woodfin Camp. 115: Adolph Suehsdorf. 116: MacQuitty International Collection. 117: Emil Muench. 118: Wim Swaan/Camera Press. 119: (top & btm rt) Ann & Bury Peerless; (btm left) Raghubir Singh. 120: Erika Stone. 121: Colour Library International. 122: Gordon Gahan. 123: Rene Burri/Magnum. 124–125: (top left) Lester Sloan/Woodfin Camp; (all others)

Gordon Gahan. 126–127: Dmitri Kessel. 128: (top) Dmitri Kessel; (btm) James Austin. 129: Dmitri Kessel. 130: Terence Spender/Colorific. 131: Kathy Clifton/John Neubauer. 132: British Tourist Authority. 133: A. F. Kersting. 134: George Mott. 135: G E Kidder Smith. 136: C M Dixon. 137: Author's collection. 138–139: (left & top rt) Inzko/Schuster; (btm rt) C M Dixon. 140–141, 142–143: Ara Guler. 144–145: Wim Swaan. 146: Charles Weckler/Image Bank. 147: Loren McIntyre. 148: Frank Aleksandrowicz. 149: Wim Swaan. 150: Michael Kirtley. 151: (top & btm rt) Sonia Halliday; (btm left) Thomas Nebbia. 152–153: Charles Weckler/Image Bank. 154: Wim Swaan. 155, 156–157: Anthony Howarth/Woodfin Camp. 158: Jehangir Gazdar/Susan Griggs Agency. 159: Government of India Tourist Office. 160–161, 162–163: Albert Squillace. 164: K. Scholz/BV. 165: Thomas Nebbia. 166: Singer Bros./Robert Harding Assocs. 167: K. Scholz/BV. 168: Paul Elek Ltd. 169: Michael Kuh. 170: H. Jörg Anders. 171: F. Thomas/BV. 172: Robert Harding Assocs. 173: Wim Swaan. 174–175: William Belknap. 176: Robert Harding Assocs. 177: Victor Englebert. 178: Jeannine le Brun/BV. 179: G. Barone/BV. 180: Joachim Messerschmidt/BV. 181: Paul Elek Ltd. 182: A. Bernhaut-Archer/BV. 183: Robert Motzkin/The Stock Shop. 184–185: Walter H. D. Müller/BV. 186: Geopress/BV. 187: Wim Swaan. 188: Paul Elek Ltd. 189: Wim Swaan. 190–191: Robert Motzkin/The Stock Shop. 192: Hans Saler/BV. 193, 194: Michael Kuh. 195: (top left & btm) Michael Kuh; (top rt) Adam Woolfitt/Woodfin Camp. 196: Japan National Tourist Organization. 197: David Westphal. 198: Peter Grilli. 199: (top) David Westphal; (btm) Peter Grilli. 200: MacQuitty International Collection. 201: C M Dixon. 202: William A. Graham. 203: (top) Sonia Halliday; (btm) Erich Hartmann/Magnum. 204–205: Ram Panjabi. 206: Wim Swaan. 207: Adam Woolfitt/Woodfin Camp. 208–209: John de Visser. 210: Colour Library International. 211: Wim Swaan. 212–213: Paul Elek Ltd. 214–215: Alterman Studios, Charleston. 216–217, 218–219: Dr. John P. Schaefer. 220–221: Wim Swaan. 222: Adolph Suehsdorf. 223: (top) Wim Swaan; (btm) Adolph Suehsdorf. 224: Joseph C. Farber. 225: Albert Squillace. 226: New York Daily News. 227: Jo Fine. 228: Japan National Tourist Organization. 229: Alfons Lutgen/BV. 230: Japan National Tourist Organization. 231: (top) Hubert Kanus/BV; (btm) Enrico Mariani/BV. 232: Donald J. Bruggink/Marcel Breuer & Assocs. 233: Marcel Breuer & Assocs. 234–235: Hedrich-Blessing, Chicago/Marcel Breuer & Assocs.